842
C615a
O33p

CONVENT OF
2100 GR
EL CAJO

D1034471

CHRISTIAN HERITAGE COLLEGE LIBRARY
2100 Greenfield Dr.
El Cajon, California 92021

PAUL CLAUDEL
and THE TIDINGS BROUGHT TO MARY

BY THE SAME AUTHOR:
Voltaire, Myth and Reality
(Cork University Press,
2nd ed. 1946). *Price* 10/6

PAUL CLAUDEL

and

"The Tidings Brought to Mary"

By *Mary Josephine*

KATHLEEN O'FLAHERTY,
M.A., Ph.D.

PREFACE BY PAUL CLAUDEL

49-1314

842.91

CORK UNIVERSITY PRESS
THE NEWMAN PRESS, WESTMINSTER, MARYLAND
1949

809
O 33

736

Published by the Cork University Press, University College,
Cork

Printed in Ireland by the Eagle Printing Works, South Mall, Cork
Printers to the Cork University Press

Préface
pour le livre de Kathleen O'Flaherty
sur l'Annonce faite à Marie

Tous les gens dont le métier est de parler en public,
acteurs, prédicateurs, conférenciers, ont constaté cet étrange
phénomène psychologique, comparable au procédé du radar,
qui leur permet de se rendre compte, par une espèce de son-
dage et de pression subtile, des dispositions de leur auditoire,
de mesurer, à chaque phrase, son degré d'accueil ou de ré-
sistance. Il en va de même, peut-être plus distinctement, pour
un auteur de lire à qui l'on apporte une traduction ou une
critique de l'une de ses œuvres. Tout à l'heure il parlait tout
seul, dans le vide, — cela m'est arrivé pendant une longue suite
d'années —, tout à coup il s'entend qu'a parlé à quelqu'un,
il y a un écran quelque part, un appareil intercepteur ou
récepteur qui lui renvoie le son de sa voix et de son âme, ac-
cepté, refusé, interprété, interrogé, diminué parfois et quelquefois
enrichi. Il passe. Il y a communication. Il y a une oreille qui
s'est posée sur lui, et pour derrière cette oreille, tout un monde
inconnu qui écoute et qui devient en quelque degré, par rap-
port à lui effet, et à qui un bienfaiteur lui a permis de s'amener
en tant que cause. Un nouveau champ de responsabilité s'est
ouvert à lui. Il s'aperçoit lui-même en tant que responsable
à l'égard d'une nouvelle qualité d'attention. L'Angleterre,
l'Allemagne, l'Italie, l'Irlande, tous ces pays, à l'instant
encore, n'étaient pour lui qu'expressions géographiques. Main-
tenant il y a contact. Tous ces pays il s'est mis à parler leur
langue: avec pas autre chose que la sienne. On a besoin de
lui en allemand, en russe, en irlandais...

C'est votre cher pays, Madame, aujourd'hui, qui au bout de

30084

vos deux bras, tend les mains, des mains délicates et savantes, à cet enfant ressuscité qu'une France réconciliée, par delà le mensonge et le reniement de Voltaire, ne cesse jamais d'offrir et de demander à tous les horizons. C'est le fils de Dieu, à qui nous donnons le vêtement sacré que l'Église lui a fait, que nos deux nations catholiques, à travers la mer, la persécution et la tempête n'ont jamais cessé de se proposer l'une à l'autre, et à qui leur amour réciproque n'a jamais cessé dans le miracle d'offrir la possibilité de recommencement. " Soyons joyeux ! ", dit ce sermon de S. Léon pape que Mara, au troisième acte de l'Annonce, lit solennellement à la forêt ensevelie. Et c'est effet, tandis que l'Angleterre, son apostasie consommée, par toutes les voix de sa sombre littérature ne cessait de déplorer le Paradis perdu, l'Irlande pauvre, opprimée, mais elle aussi invincible dans sa foi, ne perdait point le secret de la joie. Le secret de la joie divine ! De cette joie que j'ai vu rayonner aux États Unis sur le visage de tant d'excellents prêtres, de qui tout l'évangile tenait dans cette parole de leur Seigneur : je suis venu afin qu'ils aient la vie et qu'ils l'aient plus abondamment.

Paris. 4 février 1948

FOREWORD

In an essay of this scope it has not seemed necessary to give a formal bibliography. A debt to M. J. Madaule must, however, be acknowledged ; his two books, *Le Génie de Paul Claudel* and *Le Drame de Paul Claudel*, are quite indispensable. References to these works, as well as to those of Louis Gillet, M. André Molitor and other critics, will be found in the footnotes.

I have, in general, given the titles of Claudel's works in English when a translation has been published ; otherwise I have kept the French titles.

As frequent reference to all Claudel's important plays was inevitable and as many of these are not readily available at the moment, I have given in an Appendix a brief synopsis of the best known of his works.

The page references given in this book after extracts from *The Tidings Brought to Mary* are to the 81st edition, published by Gallimard. When two English versions seemed possible, as happens not infrequently in Claudel's poetry, I used, for purposes of comparison, Louise Morgan Still's translation of the play (Chatto and Windus, 1916). In as far as possible, I have endeavoured to preserve the Claudelian rhythm in the quotations which I have used. While no great poetry lends itself to a really satisfactory translation that of Claudel, governed by no fixed rules, moving to the measure of its own intimate, secret cadence, presents unusual difficulties. This is especially true when the exigencies of a critical study demand a fairly literal rendering. The attempt to give some approximation to Claudel's use of irregular lines, to his *verset*, appeared desirable since otherwise any exposition of his use of free blank verse would be impossible.

If this essay introduces even a few readers to the work of that very great modern poet, Paul Claudel, it will have fulfilled its purpose. The critic, handling such a subject, is supremely conscious that his rôle is but that of the " middleman " ; if he succeeds in passing on even a fragment, a fraction of what he has received, he has acquitted himself of his task to the best of his ability.

Before concluding, I must express my gratitude to Dr. Alfred O'Rahilly, President of University College, Cork, for his constant encouragement and invaluable suggestions ; to Professor Byrne Costigan whose discerning criticism has so greatly assisted me ; and finally, to Mademoiselle Y. Servais who first taught me to appreciate Claudel's work and without whom this study would never have been written.

I wish also to express my thanks to the Senate of the National University of Ireland for a grant towards the cost of publishing this essay.

KATHLEEN O'FLAHERTY

27th March, 1948.

CONTENTS

INTRODUCTION

IN this introduction we should like to mention some of the
reasons which caused this essay on Claudel to be published
in Ireland and to explain why, of all Claudel's numerous
works, we chose as its subject *The Tidings brought to Mary*.

Too often abroad French literature is judged by one of
two aspects : that which reflects the artificial life of the
salons, the frivolity, the irony, the preciosity of the country
of Voltaire ; or else that which consists in Rabelaisian
humour, and a thirst for pleasure. That these elements exist
in French literature is undeniable ; that they should be
assumed to represent the whole is absurd. No other nation
has proclaimed to such a high degree the love of serious and
essential things, the cult of moral greatness ; and this is
frequently accompanied by a sort of austerity very close to
asceticism. The direct result of this harsh severity towards
self has been, in one domain, the Cornelian hero athirst for
sacrifice ; in another, the amazing diversity of French saints.
Although Claudel possesses a healthy sense of humour,
although he loves the rich beauty of the world, he is essentially a member of this second group who seek the absolute.
Very recently he deplored, in his contemporaries, the
waning appreciation of great things : " They yawn at the
thought of the *Iliad*, but they go into ecstasies at the thought
of the *Chartreuse de Parme*."[1]

A great poet Claudel has restored religion to a place in
the theatre such as it has hardly held since the Middle Ages.

[1] *Revue de Paris*, December, 1947. Art. " En relisant *l'Iliade*".

In order to avoid misunderstanding, let us say now that Claudel does not owe his poetic preeminence to the fact that he is a Catholic, any more than John Keats owed his to the fact that he was a non-Catholic. A Claudel who had never known the conversion of that Christmas day in 1886 would still have been a fine poet—he would not have been the same poet. This fact requires to be stressed for very often criticism in Ireland tends to one of two extremes : either a sentimentalized belief that, if a writer be a Catholic, he must be good *as a writer* ; or a conviction that religion, as such, must be excluded from literature. Claudel, with his scorn for all which is superficial, would laugh the first contention out of court, and, indeed, time will automatically dispose of it. The second, dependent as it is on the belief that the Christian code of morals hampers a writer, he would reject far more energetically since it is infinitely more dangerous—dangerous to literature. To ignore religion means to exclude a very large part of man's preoccupations. To construct a work which is not based on the Christian code of morals in a fundamentally Christian country leads inevitably to a division between author and reader ; an essentially basic unity is shattered and two alien worlds are attempting an impossible fusion. Claudel would certainly smile, as would many Frenchmen, at the idea that the acceptance of Christianity frustrates an author, and we fancy that he would murmur: " Dante? Bossuet? Pascal? Charles Péguy? " He knows too the tragic force with which the Christian religion is endowed, the extent to which it is " a principle of contradictions " :

" Its demands, in appearance disproportionate and un-
reasonable, are nevertheless the only ones which are

compatible with our strength and our reason. They mutilate nothing ; they are catholic, that is universal ; they appeal to the whole man, to his intelligence, to his will, to his sensitiveness ; they force us into a state of permanent mobilisation against passions, against facile doubts ; and for this perpetual war all our faculties are not too much."[2]

Primarily, therefore, we present this study of Claudel because the French poet, like his contemporaries, Charles Péguy and François Mauriac, represents the great Christian literary tradition. At this time, when France is passing through a period full of anguish and incertitude, when men wonder if all her cultural riches, her contribution to European civilization are not irremediably lost, Claudel appears as a reassuring figure. His living faith is opposed to the doubt which reigns elsewhere ; his joy is an answer to contemporary defeatism and pessimism.

As well as this religious element, however, Claudel possesses singularly human qualities which have a universal appeal. His characters are actuated by motives which are applicable to any race. We could instance Anne Vercors, Jacques and Mara in the *Tidings* : their love of the land—covetous as that love is in the two young people—could be found, with superficial variants, among any agricultural people. We find it in Dostoevsky, in Thomas Hardy, in Ramuz, in Liam O'Flaherty. Thus, while remaining essentially French, Claudel is also, as are all great writers, an echo of that which is deeper than nationality. Deliberately he has made the entire world the stage for his plays : China, America, Africa, Japan, Ceylon, Spain. The most varied periods,

[2] *Positions et Propositions*, i, p.240. (Gallimard. 2nd. ed.).

from Biblical times down to our own day, are recreated by his pen. Characters of all classes, kings, princesses, popes, merchants, peasants, beggars, occupy the scene, until we are reminded of the glorious democracy of Chaucer's pilgrims.

For all these reasons it has seemed worth while to try to interpret one of his works for Irish readers.

The choice of *The Tidings brought to Mary* is perhaps more difficult to explain for ultimately it, like every other such choice, is based on personal preference. It would have been possible to give a general view of all Claudel's work ; but such a study, in a small compass, would be of necessity superficial. It seemed that by taking one play as the subject of this essay and by occasionally treating some more general aspects of Claudel's work it would be possible to give a detailed, although certainly not exhaustive, analysis of characteristics which appear to a greater or lesser extent in all his poetry. The *Tidings* is probably better suited than say the *Satin Slipper* to serve as an introduction to Claudel. While it lacks some of the sumptuously rich poetry of the later work it has a charm and a significance which are all its own. It marks moreover one of the most essential points in Claudel's dramatic evolution. He has abandoned the somewhat confused lyricism of his earlier plays ; experience has given him a surer knowledge of the human heart ; his characters are less impetuous, less violent than in the earlier works, but they are closer to us and no less living. He has moreover fully mastered his technique. The *Tidings*, at which Claudel had worked for years intermittently —there are several earlier versions—has the perfect setting, the Middle Ages, and a simple, unified structure. Finally

4

this play reveals the serenity of the poet's soul, a serenity not displayed to such an extent in the first works ; the mature Claudel can already be discovered there in his entirety.

The *Tidings* is one of those rare books to which one can return again and again. Despite its occasional obscurities, its sometimes peculiar syntax, despite the excessive length of a few of the lyrical passages, it remains a perpetual source of pleasure. To re-read it is as exhilarating as a departure on a voyage of discovery, for fresh beauties continually stir us. Each time we journey farther into the realms of the supernatural from whence we return " troubled by a strange anguish."[3]

Since the object of this study is to introduce Claudel's work to readers to whom the poet is, by the force of circumstances, little more than a name, we have deliberately quoted at length from his writings. As well as quotations from the *Tidings* we have sometimes, by way of comparison, introduced matter from his other works.[4] We have endeavoured to show the most essential characteristics of Claudelian psychology, art and philosophy. The author's confidences about the elaboration of his work and about his technique provide such an unusual lesson in esthetics that a chapter has been dedicated to them. Not only do they cast light on his complex creation but they reveal the spiritual richness of the man, his intellectual profundity, the intimate union between the poet and the Christian, his wonderful love of the world and of humanity.

. . . . .

[3] *Correspondance, Jacques Rivière et Paul Claudel*, p.4. (Plon Nourrit, 1926).
[4] For this reason too we give in an Appendix (page 122), a short summary of the contents of Claudel's principal works.

PAUL CLAUDEL

Before touching on the text we should like to refer to a few of the habitual criticisms which are voiced about Claudel.

It is true that he is often a difficult poet—that is one of the most usual complaints about his work. Yet is it not a fact that much great poetry is to some extent inaccessible to the poet's contemporaries? Every effort to achieve a renewal of old artistic forms causes some inevitable obscurity. The man of genius, be he painter, musician or poet, if he create something new, something different from accepted traditions, is exposed to incomprehension and to criticism.[5] His originality has an unwonted note, which strikes strangely on the ear. The passage of years, bringing with it a certain habit of mind, alone can make the work appear accessible.

It would seem however that Claudel's obscurity will not yield completely to time. Not that he sought it deliberately ; it is merely the normal result of that powerful synthetical inspiration which disdains to explain details. For this reason he demands of his reader " that disciplined attention, that purified, sharpened mind "[6] as the only condition necessary in order to grasp the spiritual lesson of a work of art. Claudel is himself perfectly conscious of that obscurity for which critics blame him :

> " I admit," he wrote in a letter to the abbé D., " that my most transparent works must leave, in the mind of the reader, a vague disquiet and the impression that he has not exhausted the book, that the author has not

[5] " To-day. it occurs to nobody to blame Manet for having painted pictures in Manet's style. But as long as Manet lived, he was blamed for being Manet." Mauriac, François, *Journal*, ii, p.111. (Grasset, 1937).
[6] *Revue de Paris*, 1 July, 1938. Art. " Le Festin de Pierre."

completely surrendered himself, that what is said is more than equalled by that which is merely suggested."[7]

He knows that " our perception is richer than the means we have of expressing it."[8] For the true and fundamental reason of this obscurity is that the object which he aspires to reach, God, will always escape us in a certain measure. Only by approximations shall we grasp the Infinite. When the Christian poet strives to understand men, he sees them as creatures of God; for this reason they assume a meaning only when they are re-attached to the supernatural, to the divine; for this reason their lives, their desires, their loves remain wrapped in a mystery which Claudel wishes to preserve.

We shall see that he attains to this necessary power of suggestion in his plays partly by the avoidance of introspection in his characters. Their actions are indeed motivated by the law of their own nature, but, as most often happens in real life, we are usually left to ascertain for ourselves the fundamental characteristics of the people whom he creates. Yet, even if they indulge in very little self-analysis, they sometimes, as if by chance, utter profoundly revealing words. Not in Claudel do we discover the delicate dissection of emotion which composes a Racinian tragedy; his method is both more intuitive and more purely instinctive. In a single instant, a word, a sentence, a half-articulated cry of anguish allow us to penetrate to the uttermost depths of a soul and reveal to us the intensity of a spiritual conflict.

The dramatist faces difficulties unknown to the novelist: on the stage, life must be not commented upon but pre-

[7] *Toi qui es-tu?* p.46. (Gallimard, 3rd ed.).
[8] *Ibid.*

7

sented. Thus since Claudel desired to express in poetry heavy
with imagery and symbols, the infinite depths of the human
soul, it is of course a fact that the appeal of these lyrical plays
is limited. Claudel has not created popular drama. This
does not mean that his plays are unactable. For long years
no producer would accept them ; he continued to write
without being able to form any idea of the reaction of an
audience. The disadvantages of that, from the point of
view of the dramatist, are incalculable. Henri Ghéon, for
instance, had certainly less genius than Claudel ; yet,
since he had his own company, he was immediately able
to test what he had written. This contact with the public
Claudel lacked in his early days ; his work remained too
long the creation of his imagination alone. As he remarks
somewhat sadly, in the Preface to the abridged edition of
the *Satin Slipper*, he had a long time to wait before he saw
his plays " dilated into a speaking, acting existence."[9]

The reasons for the delay in producing his plays are
readily understandable. Those responsible doubted the
dramatic appeal of Claudel's work, they feared the ample
lyricism, the strange technique of this author who appeared
to scorn all stage conventions. They feared especially the
reaction of a modern audience to the introduction of this
merveilleux chrétien : choirs of angels, resurrection from the
dead (*Tidings*) ; the apparition of St. James (Santiago), of
Prouhèze's Angel Guardian, or the statues in Prague
Cathedral which suddenly come to life (*Satin Slipper*).

The first production of *L'Otage* and of the *Tidings* was
so successful however that many of these doubts vanished.
To the general amazement Claudel's nervous, difficult

[9] *Le Soulier de Satin*, Stage edition, p.11. (Gallimard, 1943).

8

style, dense with imagery, became easy to follow on the stage. The fundamental unity of the plays, sometimes far from evident at a first reading, became very obvious, in its ordered progression, when they were acted. Even the conflicts between the characters appeared to develop a more poignant relief. The *Satin Slipper*, that very complex work, produced for the first time in 1943 by the Comédie Française[10] was an immediate and spectacular triumph.

Claudel has truly discovered the miraculous power of the written word which animates creatures of flesh and which gives life and action. If he has thus succeeded, despite the flaws in his plays from the actor's view-point, it is because of his deep understanding, his irresistible appeal and the moving beauty of his plays. In *L'Echange* Léchy Elbernon, the actress, calculating the influence which her art exerts over her audience, says: " I enter into their souls as into an empty house." Claudel himself could use the same words. Despite ourselves the poet's thought, expressed by his characters, can deeply move our spiritual being. After having read Claudel, his imagery, the beauty of his descriptions, his emotions, his beliefs, re-echo long afterwards in our innermost heart and awaken feelings, ideas and aspirations of which we had been unconscious. This he desired and sought :

" May he who hears my voice
Return home troubled and heavy."[11]

This wish is not a sign of pride ; it is simply the humble and ardent prayer of one who hopes to bear witness to God before man. For this reason, in all Claudel's plays, human

[10] In an abridged version, it is true.
[11] *Cinq grandes Odes*, pp.163-4. (Gallimard).

drama, misunderstandings, disquiet, the quest for false values, the passions of the characters, serve but to throw into more striking relief the one great problem : salvation, the response of the free being to the call of Grace. And we too, penetrated, as if despite ourselves, by this spiritual message, are continually placed, as are his characters, face to face with God.

CHAPTER I.

LIFE

> " O Wisdom formerly encountered !
> so it was you who, without my
> knowing it, before me walked
> in the days of my childhood.
> And who, when I staggered and
> fell, awaited me sadly, indul-
> gently."—*Le Fleuve*.

PAUL Claudel was born in 1868 at Villeneuve-sur-Fère-en-Tardinois where his father was, at that time, Registrar of Mortgages. Later the family moved to other country towns in the same region. There, in the heart of an agricultural district, the poet's early life was spent ; there he learned to love the nature that surrounded him. In later years, this appreciation of the beauty which is one of God's gifts to man, was to become an outstanding feature of his poetry. His reaction is never that of the city man to whom nature represents a mysterious, intangible loveliness, but that of the peasant, of the farmer. In his veins there ran the blood of men who had made their living by the soil ; in his writings is made articulate the love of the fertile earth, the joy of harvest, even bitter " land-hunger ". All this he drew from the years of his childhood, those years of which he paints a brief picture in *Connaissance de l'Est* :

> " I see myself again, in the highest fork of the old tree, in the wind, a child swaying amidst the apples. From there . . . spectator of the theatre of the world, deep in thought, I contemplate the relief and the conformation

of the earth, the disposition of slopes and of flat lands ;
. . . The moon rises, I turn my face towards her, bathed,
in this house of fruit, I remain motionless, and from
time to time an apple falls from the tree like a heavy,
ripe thought."[1]

This power to meditate upon a landscape, to savour its
spiritual content,[2] to make it his, and then to communicate
it to the reader is always in evidence in Claudel's poetry.
He does not contemplate it from a viewpoint which is solely
artistic : he seeks its profound meaning, he projects on
to it something of his emotions, his moods, his soul. Examples
too numerous to quote crowd into one's mind : the melancholy of certain oriental landscapes (*Connaissance de l'Est*) ;
the charm of the French countryside evoked by an exile
(*L'Echange*) ; the city of Rome, seen at night (*Le Père
humilié*) ; the burning beauty of tropical lands (*The Satin
Slipper*), to mention but a few.

In 1882 this country boy came with his family to live in
Paris, and Claudel attended the lycée Louis-le-Grand.
Growing up he found himself a prisoner in the " materialistic gaol " which France at that period represented. This
materialism he afterwards expressed in his trilogy, *L'Otage*,
Le Pain dur and *Le Père humilié* where it is symbolized in
the persons of the Turelures, father and son. As a boy, however, Claudel accepted the narrow mechanistic view of the

---

[1] pp.116-117. (Mercure de France).
[2] It is not, perhaps, superfluous, to point out that, while Claudel
differs essentially from Chateaubriand, the great French Romanticist,
both writers attach considerable importance to the spiritual impli-
cations of a landscape. Chateaubriand, indeed, frequently uses the
method shown in the passage quoted from *Connaissance de l'Est*: a descriptive passage into which the final phrase infuses a philosophical
meaning.

universe then prevalent ; it inspired him with little enthusiasm but it appeared to him to be the only possible
solution to many problems. It seemed to him, in its realism
and its very crudity, more honest than the elegant pessimism
of Renan ; yet, in his very early youth, like most of his
generation, he had felt the charm of the author of *La Vie
de Jésus*. Not for long however was Claudel destined to
remain confined by the philosophical ideas of his age.

If it were not to simplify unduly we could say that he was
vouchsafed three revelations. The first we have seen : his
childhood in Tardinois had imbued him with an intimate,
profound love of nature. The second came in June 1886.
The poetry of Rimbaud, that strange, wayward figure who
shed his brief superb comet-light on French literature,
brought to Claudel a vision of the infinite. He realized the
existence of another world, a world of beauty and mystery,
beyond the narrow bounds which his generation set. It was,
he says himself, the first crack in the prison wall.

The third revelation came as the result of a casual visit,
made out of artistic curiosity, to Notre-Dame Cathedral,
during Vespers on Christmas Day, 1886. There his whole
being was flooded by the knowledge, the certainty of the
existence of a personal God. Later he described this
experience in the *Magnificat* :

" And lo ! You were Somebody all of a sudden."

His conviction was instantaneous and complete ; unlike
those other great modern converts, Charles Péguy, Henri
Ghéon, Jacques Rivière, he walked no long path of doubt
and difficulty. He immediately, unhesitatingly accepted the
idea of God ; this he tells us in an often-quoted passage
from *Ma Conversion* :

" Then the event which dominates my life took place. In one instant my heart was touched and I believed. I believed with such a strength of adherence, with such a profound conviction, with such a certitude, that there was room for no sort of doubt. And since then all books, all the hazards of a troubled life, have been incapable of shaking my faith or, in truth, of touching it."[3]

If, however, he had been moved in his very soul, all the theory of life which he had built up remained intact. The site was still cluttered up with the crumbling walls of the building which had stood there. It is not easy to abandon one's beliefs, one's prejudices, one's dislike of priests, above all, one's pride. Claudel himself admits that the thought of telling his family, who had abandoned all religious practice, and his friends, amongst whom there was not a single Catholic, was the chief cause which delayed an avowal of his changed beliefs. After that moment at Notre-Dame four long years passed before Claudel returned to the Sacraments. In the *Hound of Heaven* Francis Thompson tells us of his flight to escape God ; in the *Magnificat* Claudel makes somewhat similar revelations of the violence of that struggle :

" And I was before You like a wrestler who bends,
Not that he thinks himself weak but because the other is stronger."

During these four years Claudel's ordinary life continued. He attended the Ecole du Droit and the Ecole des Sciences Politiques and entered the French diplomatic service. Then began his existence as a wanderer, an exile whose thoughts were continually, nostalgically returning to the Tardinois

[3] *Ma Conversion*. Text republished in *Comment lire Paul Claudel*, Jouve, Raymond, p.81. (Ed. aux Etudiants de France, 1945).

scenes of his childhood, to that land where " the garden is perfumed and all the birds sing in French ".[3a] In 1893 he set out for America where he was stationed first in New York and later in Boston.

He had already written three plays : the rich, tempestuous, exuberant *Tête d'Or, La Ville* and, in 1892, the first version of the *Tidings brought to Mary, La jeune fille Violaine.* His next production, *L'Echange*, was inspired by America. In 1895 he was transferred to China and there, in the solitude of a secret, alien, ancient land, he wrote what is perhaps his finest prose work, *Connaissance de l'Est.* From the same period dates *Le Repos du Septième Jour* where his preoccupation with the supernatural achieves a higher degree of serenity than had appeared in his earlier works. For the second time he re-wrote *La jeune fille Violaine* and began the first of his *Cinq grandes Odes,* " Les Muses ". After a voyage to France in 1900 he returned again to the East. Five years later he married Reine-Sainte-Marie Perrin, the daughter of an architect. It is certain that Pierre de Craon's lyrical praise of architecture in the *Tidings* owes much to this family connection.

In 1903-4 he composed those austere studies : *Connaissance du Temps* and *Traité de la Co-naissance au Monde et de Soi-même* where he outlined his philosophy and his artistic theories. In 1906 he wrote *Partage de Midi*, a passionate play, vibrating with lyrical intensity, where the problem of two lovers is posed with remarkable force. During the years which followed, other works were being prepared, some-

---

[3a] It is curious to find the following line in a poem in Scots Gaelic :
" An uair bha Gàilig aig na h-eòin."
(" When all the birds in Gaelic sang ")—*Linn an Aigh* by J. Mac Cuaraig.

times simultaneously, as for instance, the remaining four of the *Cinq grandes Odes* or certain of the liturgical poems which, in 1916, appeared in the volume *Corona Benignitatis Anni Dei*. These years too saw the beginning of that remarkable *Correspondance avec Jacques Rivière*, published only in 1926.

His career led him to visit the most diverse countries. Successively he held official appointments at Prague, at Frankfort, at Hambourg. During the war of 1914-1918 he passed through Sweden, Norway, England ; he spent some time in Italy and in Brazil. After the Armistice he was sent to Denmark and then, as Ambassador, to Tokio. Later in Washington he negotiated the Kellog-Briand Pact. Finally he terminated his official career in Brussels in 1935 :

> " The diplomat," he writes himself, " never knows where he will be to-morrow. The Goddess Administration transports him and suddenly deposits him in the most unexpected, the most diverse places, all over the atlas. He falls asleep in Denmark and it is in a landscape of palm trees and pagodas that he awakens, rubbing his eyes, not surprised but interested."[4]

Thus, during the period of his greatest poetic activity Claudel was far from inhabiting an ivory tower ; he had a most active and successful life in a career which, on the surface, appears to present a profound contrast with his imaginative work. This recluse moved in " society " ; this lyric poet sent in detailed and factual reports about such unlikely subjects as agriculture in China.[5] But this contrast

---

[4] *Contacts et Circonstances*, p.63. (Gallimard, 1940).

[5] It was at the time that he was composing his *Odes* that he wrote to Arthur Fontaine : " It is a real joy for me to touch all those very big, very real things, trams, sewers, electricity and pitiless accountancy." 9th Dec., 1906. Letter quoted in *Toi, qui es-tu?* p.99. (Gallimard, 3rd ed.).

is only apparent : Claudel would indignantly repudiate the doctrine which holds that a poet must withdraw himself from ordinary life in order the better to follow his vocation. For he, most mystical of modern poets, knows full well the inevitable failure awaiting all art which ignores the common humanity of man. Not content with discovering the hidden meaning of landscapes, he forced himself to understand the peoples whom he visited : their customs, their traditions, the originality of their art, their fundamental nature—in a word, their soul.

The successive adaptations rendered necessary by his career, the very active nature of his life in no way interfered with his creative work. In 1910, at Prague, he finished *L'Otage* ; in 1911, the *Cantate à trois Voix* ; in 1912, the third and final version of *La jeune fille Violaine*, *The Tidings brought to Mary* ; in 1913 a satirical play, *Protée*. During the war he wrote the sequel of *L'Otage*, two plays, *Le Pain dur* and *Le Père humilié*, thus composing a trilogy. At the same time he wrote his *Poèmes de Guerre*, *La Messe là-bas* and some of the poems of his *Feuilles de Saints*. In Brazil, towards 1919, he began his *Satin Slipper* at which he worked for five years. After that came a considerable number of prose works : discussions on art and literature, notes on his travels, reflections on life such as *L'Oiseau noir dans le Soleil levant*, *Positions et Propositions* (2 vols.), *Conversations dans le Loir-et-Cher* or *Introduction à la Peinture Hollandaise*.

More and more however religious subjects attracted him and occupied an essential place in the work of his later years. He has published a whole series of books where meditations on Biblical texts are mingled with the author's thoughts about the world and men, with his personal memories. Such are *Figures et Paraboles*, *Les Aventures de Sophie*, *Introduction au " Livre de Ruth "*, *Un Poète regarde la Croix*, *L'Epée et le Miroir*, *Présence et Prophétie*. It is at Brangues, whither he retired after his long career, that Claudel, renouncing his creative work, thus devoted himself to Biblical studies.

On 13th March, 1947 he became a member of the French Academy. The nomination was long over-due : just twelve years ago this assembly had shocked France by preferring to Paul Claudel the novelist Claude Farrère. But this tardy tribute hardly interrupts the poet's solitude on the peaceful banks of the Rhône. After his life's wandering he contemplates about him " the sad river of memories, of images and of ideas "[6] but he feels " elsewhere, beneath, a little lower."[7] Far from the stir of existence but linked in spiritual union to his fellow-men " he draws away from ephemeral things in order to fill his mind only with that which does not pass."[8] With serenity he awaits death :

> " It is there, under an old wall covered with moss and maidenhair fern, that I have marked out my place. It is there, hardly separated from the countryside and its toils, that I shall rest beside that little innocent child that I have lost and to whose grave I often come to say my rosary."[9]

[6] *Un Poète regarde la Croix*, p.234.
[7] *Ibid.* p.235.
[8] Gillet, Louis, *Claudel présent*, p.16. (Egloff, 1943).
[9] *Pages de Prose* (edited by André Blanchet), pp.65-6. (Gallimard, 1944).

CHAPTER II.

THE PLOT OF THE *TIDINGS*

> " Life, for [the Christian], is not an incoherent series of vague, incomplete gestures, but a precise drama which has a *dénouement* and a meaning."—(*Positions et Propositions*).

THE *Tidings* is a strange play where drama is transformed into a Mystery ; the conflict of souls is followed by their pacification and their transformation through Grace. When human love fails, the characters are spiritualized as a result of sorrow. The curve of the action corresponds admirably to the subtle definition of M. J. Madaule :

" We see the imperfect harmony of the beginning being followed by a series of dissonances which form the magic element in the perfect harmony of the conclusion."[1]

This play is, as we saw, Claudel's third handling of the same subject. It would certainly be interesting to follow its evolution ; but the limits of this study permit us to make only a few remarks. The transformation lies less in the alteration of the period (the setting of the first two plays is modern) or of minor details, less in the introduction of new elements or even characters than in a greater spiritualization of the whole atmosphere and above all of the heroine. In the earlier versions she is merely an exquisite young girl

[1] *Le Génie de Paul Claudel*, p.297. (Desclée De Brouwer).

who renounces human happiness. In the *Tidings* her solitude is more tragic and complete ; her suffering and her sacrifice assume to a greater extent the aspect of an expiation for the sins of others.

The action takes place towards the end of the Middle Ages, a period when the piles of the great Gothic cathedrals were rising, their laced spires clear-cut against the sky ; a period of divisions and political crises, of heresy and of treason ; but a period too whose loyalty and faith were to be symbolized by the slender figure of Jeanne, the Maid of Orleans.

It is just before daybreak when the curtain rises for the Prologue ; daybreak in Spring, but the big barn at Combernon is shadowy and dark. Young Violaine Vercors has come to pardon Pierre de Craon, the architect, whom God had stricken with the scourge of leprosy as a punishment for his attempt upon the girl. Having urged him to be resigned Violaine, because she is happy and young and full of compassion, kisses him innocently. Pierre's character is profoundly altered in this third and final version of the subject. In the second version of *La jeune fille Violaine* (he did not appear in the first) Pierre is guilty of no sin. On the contrary, having himself heard the imperious call of God, he communicates a similar call to Violaine. The final choice of Claudel is happier : two saints in one play seems somewhat exaggerated !

In the first Act Anne Vercors, the master of Combernon, sets out on a pilgrimage for Jerusalem. His absence is an essential factor in the action. Because of it, he hands over Combernon to Jacques, thus exciting Mara's jealousy. Had he been present, while Violaine would probably have contracted leprosy, he would have protected her interests and overcome Mara's intrigues. Before Anne's departure he betrothes Violaine, his elder daughter, to his employee, Jacques Hury, to whom he also entrusts his land. But later Mara, the younger girl, who secretly loves Jacques and covets Combernon, accuses Violaine of infidelity towards him who is to be her husband. From a hiding place she had seen her sister's compassionate kiss given to the leper. When her insinuations to Jacques fail she forces her mother to bear a message to Violaine : on the day of her sister's wedding she will hang herself. Meanwhile Violaine has contracted leprosy and, when she tells Jacques, he curses her and himself leads her away to the distant wood of Géyn. Jacques marries Mara and a little daughter, Aubaine, is born to them.

In the third Act which takes place eight years later, on Christmas Eve, Mara, carrying the dead body of her child, goes to seek Violaine, the blind leper, so that she, the holy recluse, may work a miracle. This part of the play underwent a considerable transformation. Violaine in the first two versions is a blind recluse. The poor come to her ; she re-establishes peace in disunited families ; she heals the sick ; she restores the sight of Aubain—a nephew, not a niece—who has been blind from birth. In the *Tidings* she works a single miracle, but it is more striking, more wonderful than those of *La jeune fille Violaine*. At Mara's supplications Violaine at last agrees to pray and her pain-filled life, her humility obtain from God the resurrection of the little girl. But a change has come : Aubaine's eyes had been black like her mother's, they are now the blue eyes of Violaine.

This miracle which she works in the *Tidings* merely serves to exasperate Mara's jealousy and hatred: Jacques has never ceased to love Violaine in his heart, now the little daughter seems to have become in part her child. Mara sets a trap for her sister; crushing her beneath a cart-load of sand she wounds her mortally. Pierre de Craon, healed long since of his leprosy, bears her to Combernon where, having convinced Jacques of her innocence, she dies radiating about her gentleness and peace.

.   .   .   .   .

The structure of the play attains to a unity and perfection which are rare in Claudel's dramatic works. In *L'Otage*, for instance, the action is often melodramatic; here it is re-strained[2] and the psychological situations are, on the whole, likely. *Le Père humilié* ends with an effusion of somewhat ill-defined emotions; in the *Tidings*, the conclusion is clear and simple. However rich the subject matter and poetry of the *Satin Slipper* may be, it remains true that this great historical fresco has a complex and sometimes confused sequence of scenes; here, on the contrary, the action is progressive and clear.

Everything converges towards Violaine and the evolution of the play follows the different phases of her spiritual transformation: Violaine the happy young girl; Violaine, betrothed; Violaine, the leper recluse; Violaine, injured and dying; Violaine dead, a living victim. Despite the transparently calm atmosphere of the play, the action is eminently tragic and is marked by brutal or disastrous

[2] The healing of Pierre de Craon and the resurrection of the child must, in this play of the Middle Ages, be accepted for what they are: miracles.

22

events : Pierre's attack, of which we hear ; the breaking-off of Violaine's engagement ; Mara's crime. If the conflicts are less violent than in Claudel's other plays we see nevertheless how poignant is the clash between the characters, the defeat of all human designs. Man, an unhappy, imperfect creature, subject to numerous limitations, is torn between his desire for God and for the things of the earth. Everything depends on his liberty :

" It is the source of our merits and the justification of our punishment. Whether, therefore, the Christian consider Nature ; whether he descend into himself or whether he raise his eyes towards God, he ceaselessly perceives a series of conflicts and of contradictions which can be resolved into final harmony only by the intervention of his personal will."[3]

Lastly, as a background to this intimate drama of a family we see the dark picture of the decline of the Middle Ages, one of the most troubled periods of history.

[3] Madaule, Jacques, *Le Génie de Paul Claudel*, p.290. (Desclée De Brouwer).

CHAPTER III.

THE HISTORICAL BACKGROUND

> " It is the time of Joan of Arc, of
> crisis and of suffering and also of
> the renaissance of the mother-
> land, a twilight between two
> ages."—*Claudel-Péguy*, Louis Gillet.

" THE whole play," Claudel states, " takes place at the
end of conventional Middle Ages." Does he wish, by
this, to express his contempt for the celebrated Romantic
" local colour " or is it merely one of those mocking remarks which he so readily inserts in his stage directions?[1]
However that may be, it is certain that the background of
the play, the period of the Middle Ages, is very real and
very true, reconstructed by a mind, a heart, an imagination
which are profoundly Catholic.

This does not mean that the *Tidings* is strictly speaking an
historical play. *L'Otage* for example is more deserving of
that title. Since Claudel's interest is in souls rather than in
things, he does not attempt to reproduce in detail here a
picture of the events of the period any more than he gives
prominence to its great figures. It is as a poet that he
desired to depict the atmosphere of the age and the historical setting counts only in so much as it enriches the
meaning of the psychological drama or recalls the religious
life of an epoch of deep faith. And so only intermittently
does Claudel present in the background of the play the

[1] Cf. *Satin Slipper*.

period where the drama takes place. Sometimes he employs stage indications, for instance, the description of the barn at Combernon with its pillars that support a vaulted roof, with its heavy door on which are painted crude images of the saints ; or again that of the big farm kitchen and its great fireplace with an emblazoned hood. On other occasions the words of the characters present the historical setting. Thus in their picturesque conversation the people of Chevoche, on Christmas Eve, recall the exploits of Joan of Arc and, overjoyed, they visualize the triumphant arrival of the King at Rheims. Anne Vercors it is who most often describes the manners, customs and events ; the political, social and religious situations of the period.

Combernon, the domain his ancestors have held since the time of St. Genevieve, had been a pagan land which the Vercors christianized. It is free of all taxes and the only duty of its inhabitants is to pay tithes to the recluses who dwell in the monastery of Monsanvierge. Life on the farm is simple, rustic, patriarchal : meals are shared in common by masters and servants ; everything betokens a noble hospitality, a love of the land, a devotion to tradition and to duty ; all are respectful of the authority of the master, Anne. The group seems indeed to belong to a period of the Middle Ages more remote than the 15th century. The cult of the past, Anne's strong personality, the influence of Monsanvierge have preserved inviolate a life of faith which everywhere else tends to disappear. Prayer in common comes naturally to these people who live the liturgy of the Church. Anne, despite his age, sets out on a hazardous pilgrimage. Pierre, not a member of the family but moving within its sphere of influence, remains a builder of churches, those magnificent houses of God constructed from earthly materials to shelter the infinite. In this conception of architecture we find once again the spirit of the Middle Ages. These edifices are the wonderful expression of the collective faith of a whole people. St. Justice at which Pierre and his workers toil patiently, lovingly, for ten years is paid for by the guilds of Rheims and by the great ladies of the district who contribute their jewels.

" Firstly, as a thank-offering to God for seven fat summers
    while distress reigned everywhere else in the kingdom,
For abundant grain and fruit, for cheap and beautiful
    wool,
For cloth and parchment profitably sold to the mer-
    chants of Paris and Germany.
Secondly, for the liberties acquired, the privileges
    conferred by our Lord the King,
The old order issued against us by Bishops Felix II and
    Abondant de Cramail
Rescinded by the Pope." (p.20).

Whether as an act of thanksgiving or as a manifestation of the faith of a people, the spires of splendid cathedrals arise everywhere towards the sky. And Pierre, the architect, is not alone in his enthusiasm for their beauty ; it is shared by the humblest apprentice. All, master and men, work harmoniously together at this great task, each one bringing to it his intelligence, his heart, his love of God.

If, however, as we saw, Combernon had escaped the misfortunes of the time, nevertheless to this oasis there come painful echoes of a menaced, threatened world. At this period of crisis the old order was yielding before the impact of new forces ; already the strange outlines of another era could be glimpsed. At the opening of the play, the world beyond Combernon appears to represent only incoherence and division. The Church is split by the great Schism ; the major heresies can be foreseen ; Constantinople is in the hands of the Turks and all Europe, the whole Christian civilization, is menaced.

As for France, invaded by the English, ravaged by the Hundred Years' War, her very existence is in peril. At Combernon Anne is the only one who seems to realize the misfortunes which weigh upon his country :

> " But you at least see that everything is upset, out of its
> rightful place, and that each man seeks desperately
> to find where that place is.
> And that smoke which you see sometimes in the distance
> does not come from the burning of mere straw.
> And those great crowds of poor people who come to us
> from all sides.
> There is no longer a King reigning in France, as the
> Prophet predicted." (p.45).

Pest, famine, and war decimate the population and a bitter pessimism reigns. In the midst of this collapse there remains only the weak king of Bourges

> " so small that he cannot be seen amidst the reeds of the
> Loire." (p.45).

Anne it is too who measures the peril which menaces Christendom :

> " In place of the Pope we have three Popes and in place
> of Rome some council or other in Switzerland.
> All is struggle and movement,
> Since there is no longer any counter-weight to keep it
> in position." (pp.45-46).

In the third Act a period of eight years has elapsed since the opening and all has changed in France. On that strange Christmas Eve, in the cave at Géyn, Mara reads the Office while Violaine clasps in her arms the body of little Aubaine. Then in the stillness far-off trumpets sound to announce the passage of the King who, led by Jeanne D'Arc, journeys towards Rheims. From the heart of Lorraine the unknown child had come to save France. By making her pass thus during this vital scene, Claudel links, in our imagination, these two daughters of the French soil who, one by action, one by humble suffering, strive for the spiritual salvation of France. The arrival of the heroic seventeen year old girl who rides beside the King is hailed by shouts of joy and this acclamation is linked to the lonely triumph in the icy cave where, at the prayer of the leper, God restores life to the dead child. Violaine's sacrifice passes beyond the bounds of Combernon. She helps to save her own family, but she also helps to save a world menaced with destruction. The joy of Christmas symbolizes the victory of God. After Jeanne's martyrdom at Rouen, after Violaine's death, the world gradually rediscovers stability: " The King and Pope are once more restored to France and the Universe." (p.194). Disorder vanishes, justice begins to reign again ; the world has emerged from a troubled age ; the Church, ever young and vital, finds fresh strength and unity ; man faces a new future. In its psychological and tragic development the play seems to follow the same line as historical events. The peace which dominates the conclusion of the *Tidings* is linked to the salvation of France and of Christendom at a period so like our own when all moral and spiritual values had appeared to be in danger.

Thus through the introduction of this historical element Claudel extends the scope of his play. Thus too does he show that the forces of evil—disasters, discord, all the tragic upheavals of world history—can be mitigated, transmuted, sometimes averted by the prayer, the abnegation of often humble, apparently insignificant individuals; hidden spiritual powers exert their influence when man is too sorely tried.

CHAPTER IV.

VIOLAINE AND PIERRE DE CRAON

> " Is it true that I am your God? Did
> you think to escape Me so easily?
> Despite all that I have done
> against you, is it so easy to avoid
> loving Me? "—(*La Messe là-bas*).

IN the Prologue, when Violaine comes to open the heavy
door of the barn at Combernon for Pierre, she appears in
all the freshness and spontaneity of youth. She is a charm-
ing, simple, gently mischievous girl. She listens with naïve
wonder to the beautiful legend of Saint Justice which Pierre
tells her. Yet her gaiety surpasses that which we normally
expect to find even in one who is looking forward confi-
dently to life, enjoying the beauty of the world, the sweetness
of loving and of being loved. It is the bliss of a pure soul,
full of trust in God. Brought face to face with Pierre's
sorrow, her delight makes her somewhat ashamed :

" Forgive me for being too happy ! Because he whom I
love

Loves me, and I am sure of him, and I know that he
loves me, and everything is equal between us !

And because God made me for happiness and not for
evil nor for any suffering." (p.29).

Yet this exuberance often gives place to greater gravity
and greater maturity. Her father, the old patriarch, sees
clearly the successive transformations which occur in this

apparently uncomplex character. On his return, after Violaine's death, he evokes her image as she already, unknowing, journeyed towards sorrow :

> " And little by little the impetuous mischievousness of
>   the laughing child
> Melted into the emotions of a young maiden, into
>   suffering and the heaviness of love, and already, when
>   I left,
> I saw in her eyes, amidst those spring blossoms, one
>   unknown bloom." (p.204).

Even in the Prologue, Violaine's joy at being loved is troubled by a vague uneasiness. Jacques' gift, the beautiful ring which she sacrifices in order to aid in the construction of the Cathedral of St. Justice, frightens her a little. Does she foresee the fragility of human happiness? The " laughing child " walks already towards mystery and its shadow touches her, albeit lightly. Normally, she should strive to avoid this man ; but Violaine fears neither carnal desires nor leprosy even though Pierre has told her of the possible terrible contagion of the illness : " God is there Who can protect me " (p.15), is her only answer. And this is far from being the carelessness of a young girl. When, fully aware of the gravity of Pierre's sin, she pardons him ; when she pities the solitude of the leper ; when she tries to restore his faith in his vocation as a church-builder ; when she appeals to his spirit of sacrifice, Violaine is, in her lucidity, her gentleness and her kindness, a serious, grave woman.

Perhaps, too, she realizes that innocently, unconsciously, she tempted Pierre. Her mother describes her attitude during his previous visit :

" And she, while he spoke,
　　How she listened to him, her eyes wide like a simpleton,
　　Forgetting to serve the drink so that I had to get cross
　　　with her ! " (p.42).

Violaine at that time was only sixteen ; to her Pierre was
the poet, the wanderer who could tell tales of romance and
delight ; the man whose life was spent in raising prayerful
spires. But, although she did not realize it, Pierre was in
love with her and the engrossed attention with which she
listened to his words could not but give him hope and
increase his passion. At the end of the play, after her death,
Pierre addresses her :

" O Violaine ! O woman through whom comes temp-
　　tation ! " (p.208).

However this may be, certain it is that, during this opening
scene, childishness and maturity are strangely mingled in
Violaine. In many respects she is already a soul apart.

.　　　.　　　.　　　.　　　.　　　.

In the second version of *La jeune fille Violaine* Pierre is
merely a strange messenger of God. Feeling that he must
himself cast aside earthly things and live in greater solitude,
he glimpses the richness of Violaine's soul. She is but a happy
girl and he comes to her to tell her, in prophetic tone, of
sacrifice, of abnegation, of purely earthly love " which is
like the humiliation of death ". He feels no passion for her :
she is simply the symbol of a beauty which he must renounce
in order to draw closer to God.

In the *Tidings* Pierre's rôle is transformed and becomes
far more complex. He desires Violaine ; the flames which

devour his heart are those which scorched that of Mesa in *Partage de Midi*. Both men are creatures of passion, impetuous and violent. In *Partage de Midi* however the focal point is the weakness and the carnal love of Mesa ; whereas, in the *Tidings*, as if Claudel desired to maintain its atmosphere of transparent purity and freshness, Pierre's sin is not shown, it precedes the action of the play. Already, when we first see him he has attained to that self-knowledge which is the beginning of holiness. It is only from Pierre himself and from Violaine's references that we learn of his temptation and of his violent assault :

> " Poor Pierre ! You didn't even succeed in killing me
> With your wretched knife. Nothing except a little cut on
> my arm which nobody noticed." (p.10).

The temptation, even if it be not yet completely sublimated, is in the past ; and, although he is still bitterly jealous of Jacques, Pierre de Craon is on the threshold of a new life, his face already illumined by the light of the supernatural.

He himself feels that Violaine is a being apart, predestined to great things. This he believes not only because God has punished his sin against her so heavily but especially because he realizes the beauty of her soul, the splendour of her charity. When he gazes on the loveliness of the spring dawn his pain-bowed spirit experiences a little peace. Almost unconsciously a hymn wells up in his heart and finds expression, a hymn of thanksgiving :

> " *Pax tibi.*
> How the whole creation is at one with God in a profound mystery !
> That which was hidden becomes visible again with Him

CONVENT OF THE SACRED HEART
2100 GREENFIELD DRIVE
EL CAJON, CALIFORNIA

736

and I feel on my face a breath bearing the freshness
of roses.

Praise your God, blessed earth, in tears and in darkness ! " (p.18).

In this morning light Violaine no longer appears to him as
a creature of flesh and blood ; he sees her in the dazzling
radiation of her purity. He humbles himself, he accepts
his punishment, his ever-increasing solitude. Before him
there lies a life of toil and sorrow but already he looks
forward to freedom-bearing death and eternity :

" The man who in his heart has preferred God sees, when
he dies, that Angel who was watching over him.

The time will come soon when another door melts
away.

When he who has pleased but few here below falls
asleep, his work finished, sheltered by the eternal and
divine Wings.

When already through translucent walls appears on all
sides dark Paradise.

And when the censers of the night mingle their perfume
with the odour of the filthy wick which is being
extinguished." (pp.18-9).

And the sinner, overwhelmed by the recollection of his
evil, in the presence of her whom he strove to harm, is
suddenly " struck by an idea ". He gives to Violaine a
foreglimpse of the demands of God's love, a knowledge of
the possibility for her of a call to a higher vocation. God
makes use of a humbled sinner in order to enlighten an
angelic and pure child.[1]

[1] Here we see an aspect of Pierre which was much more strongly
stressed in the second version of *La jeune fille Violaine*.

But while Violaine, this " little lark of France ", can fly directly heavenwards, Pierre remains too attached to earth : " In order to rise a little " he needs " the whole structure of a cathedral and all its foundations." (p.29) To serve as a link with God he has only his very earthly mission : the slow, long task of the church-builder. His loneliness is intense : is he not a leper, who knows himself to be " rotting away during life "? The evil is moral as well as physical for he still feels the terrible weight of the flesh crushing down his soul. He is alone with his human weakness, with the possibility of a new temptation, for " this diseased flesh has not healed the affected soul" (p.30). Violaine, " image of eternal beauty ", is destined to belong to another, and never will he know the sweetness of a simple life in a happy home :

> " So many proud roof-ridges ! Shall I never see that of my
> little house amidst the trees.
> So many spires whose moving shadows write the hour
> across a whole town ! Shall I never design an oven
> and a children's room? " (p.32).

His bitter complaint echoes that of Claudel in *Connaissanec de l'Est* :

> " Separation is irremediable ... It will never be granted
> me to establish my foot on immovable ground, to build
> with my hands a dwelling of stone and wood, to eat in
> peace food cooked on the domestic hearth."[2]

For the poet himself faced the bitter necessity of detachment. This world is a world of exile where man can find no permanent abode ; only when he has fully realized this

[2] p.185. (Mercure de France).

fundamental impermanency does he turn resolutely towards God and eternity.

Pierre faces the life before him courageously. He will continue to lead the existence of a workman, sleeping on a bundle of straw, eating only the simplest food, isolated from his fellows. Thus he will build the church of St. Justice under whose arches he will pour " the gold of morning ", a light which is akin to that of the human soul.

Later, miraculously healed, he feels that his sin is forgiven. Moreover, though, in the Prologue, earthly desire was still unextinguished, the disappearance of his leprosy marks the end of temptation, " woman has no power over his soul" (p.176). Conscious of the disproportion between his human wretchedness and the infinity of divine pity, he journeys towards the spiritual, mysteriously upheld by the invisible presence of Violaine who has assumed the weight of his sin.

When we next hear of him he is toiling feverishly, piously, lovingly at the construction of his cathedral, Saint Justice. He gives to his art a spiritual meaning : a church becomes a symbol of the soul in the state of Grace serving as the temple of God. The one-time leper has become an apostle amongst his workmen. He teaches them that the art of the builder cannot alone suffice : prayer and meditation are also necessary :

" For the pagan artist did everything from the exterior, and we do everything from the interior like bees,

And as the soul works on the body, nothing is inert, everything lives.

Everything is an act of thanksgiving." (p.122).

The death of Violaine leaves him strangely calm. Passion

is extinct in him ; there is " no more desire of the flesh in his heart". The dying girl represents for this convert only a wonderful spiritual force :

> " And in my arms the perfume of paradise breathed forth
> from this broken tabernacle." (p.197).

Looking back he knows now that everything began that morning at dawn in the barn of Combernon. There, from the lips of Violaine, he heard the call of God ; for him it represented that indefinable moment when the sinner already, unconsciously, turns away from evil :

> " O Violaine ! O woman through whom comes temp-
> tation,
> For not yet knowing what I should do, I looked at that
> place where your gaze rested." (p.208).

Painfully he set out along the path which she had shown him and, at the end of the play, he has travelled far.

He who, in the Prologue, was mad with despair no longer dreams of death. When he looks at the past, when he contemplates his lonely life, it all becomes, for him, a source of joy. His leprosy, his loss of Violaine were liberations which made him more fully conscious of his vocation : to raise heavenwards from the earth of men the spires of his splendid cathedrals. The man is eliminated ; there remains only the artist who, without pride, measures the extraordinary gifts which God has given to him. Not only has he received the " sense of the three dimensions " which enables him to achieve perfect harmony in his buildings ; he has also been granted the art of " working from within ", of infusing a soul into his creations. For him the stone is living, beauti-ful, flexible in the architect's hands. The churches, his

" daughters ", have arisen ; each one different from its sisters, each as individual as a human being. Ecstatically happy, full of gratitude to God Who gave him such a proud vocation, he chants his joy and his peace. All his affection goes towards St. Justice, his " most beautiful daughter ", for this cathedral is mysteriously united to the sacrifice and death of Violaine. It is for this reason that he carves the image of the dead girl at the summit of his last spire :

> " Thus at its highest point in the open sky I shall place this other Justice,
> Violaine, the leper, in all her glory, Violaine, the blind in the sight of all.
> And I shall present her, her hands crossed on her breast . . .
> And her eyes blindfolded . . .
> So that, unseeing, she may the better listen
> To the noise of the town and of the fields, and the voice of man and the voice of God at the same time." (p.200).

The grace of God turned this despairing man into a consoler. Formerly Violaine, by evoking the beauty of his art, had shown him the value of life ; now he in his turn by describing the splendour of agriculture, comforts Anne and Jacques. Violaine's sacrifice and her " vocation, like that of a solemn lily for death ", bathe his soul in a profound peace. Beneath the gaze of his little spiritual sister he will continue to live, drawing ever closer to God. Despite his sin, despite his hatred of Jacques, despite his bitterness, Pierre had all the possibilities of a fruitful soul ; this Violaine had perceived from the beginning. His nature was potentially rich and it is because of this that he rises so high ; the sinner becomes a mystic, lost in the love of Christ :

" Indeed, I have always believed that joy was a goodly
    thing,
But now, I have everything !
The act of thanksgiving loosens the stone of my heart !
Let me live thus ! let me grow thus, mingled with my
    God like the vine and the olive tree ! " (p. 209).

CHAPTER V

VIOLAINE AND ANNE VERCORS

> " Death comes . . . there he is stripped
> of all things, there he is naked
> beneath the severe look."—*Art
> Poétique.*

AT the opening of the play Anne Vercors is on a far
higher spiritual plane than Pierre for he is already
very close to God. Thus his ascension is less strikingly
evident. This grave, just, authoritative but very human man
is a tower of strength at Combernon. Just as Pierre's
churches are, to him, almost living entities, so for Anne the
land on which he lives is like a being, a close friend :

" I never cease to see the land as if it were a stable sky all
   coloured with changing tints,
   This, having a form as individual as a person, is always
      here-present with me." (p.207).

The old peasant who patiently observes the quality of the
light, the line of the fields, the rhythm of the seasons, all the
changing wonder of nature, is profoundly aware of the
delicate beauty, the superb majesty of the land. A deep
harmony unites the soul of this poet—this unconscious poet
—to the nature which God created and which reflects some
of the divine splendour of its Maker. As well, the land
represents for him a means of fulfilling his vocation and his
destiny. Ploughing and sowing have been his life task.
Yet after hard toil he has known the joy of harvest, the
pride in fertile soil ; the humble gratitude to God, " our

Companion in all the days of labour." (p.62). He has too to comfort him the knowledge that his life has been both full and loyal.

Anne Vercors' character, his spiritual existence, his faith are influenced and moulded by this harmony which exists between him and the land. From it he draws wisdom, humility and a total, blind submission to God:

" The sun and I, side by side,
     We have worked, and the result of our work is not our
          business." (p.203).

In the beauty and fertility of Combernon the old farmer sees the result of the faith, of the slow patient labour of his ancestors. They have transformed a barren, pagan soil into a fruitful Christian land. The past is closely linked with the present. Heir to a noble tradition Anne has fully understood and accepted his mission. This mission he bequeathes to Jacques Hury:

" Give food to all creatures : to men and to animals ; to the
          spirit and the body and to immortal souls." (pp.62-3).

His is an intensely living faith. He pardons fully those who offend against him; when a peasant is caught stealing his wood he orders that another bundle be given to him. His conception of the duties of fatherhood is not only noble and generous, it is also profoundly Christian. To him its most important aspect is the spiritual union which exists between parent and child. As he says to Violaine in the presence of his household:

" My soul does not part from the soul which I have
          communicated.
     What I gave cannot be returned." (p.64).

He is completely resigned to God's will. Already, when he leaves for Jerusalem, he has accepted with serenity the thought of the inevitable deprivations of old age, for " there is a time to take and a time to allow to be taken ". Despite his love of the land which has for so long been his he does not hesitate, he hands it over to the young.

While Elizabeth, his wife, is a simple being, preoccupied with everyday, personal worries,[1] Anne contemplates with troubled gaze the spectacle of his country rent by the Hundred Years' War, of Christendom in danger. This farmer sees beyond the peaceful bounds of Combernon and his heart is saddened by the " great misfortune " that weighs on the Kingdom of France. He alone appears conscious of the chaos of the dying Middle Ages and of the underlying causes of so much anarchy and suffering. These causes are lack of faith and greed for the material things to which man clings as if he had created them instead of having merely received them in trust from God. The old order is vanishing. Anne, like the Pope in *Le Père humilié*, could say :

" He Who came, it is as if He had not come. Everything which has been said, it is as if it had not been said ; everything which has been heard, it is as if it had not been heard."[2]

[1] Elizabeth, although she appears but little, is a living, real figure. A simple woman, completely dedicated to the care of her family, she fails almost entirely to understand the mysticism of the husband to whom she is so tenderly attached. She has all the intuitive perspicacity of the peasant and she thus grasps the idea of possible developments from the interplay of the characters of those around her. She does not indulge in abstractions : if she yields to Mara it is because, unhesitatingly and unerringly, she realizes the violence of her younger daughter. She accepts the fact, not because it is right but because it *is* a fact.
[2] p.88. (Gallimard, 6th ed.).

In the first version of *La jeune fille Violaine*, Anne, having completed his task at Combernon, leaves home to travel. Foreign lands and especially the sea exercise a strange fascination over him. In the second version he goes to America where his extravagant and erratic brother has just died and left his wife and children in want. In the *Tidings* his departure assumes a purely spiritual significance. When Anne decides to journey forth he is partly actuated by a desire to aid, through prayer and sacrifice, in the salvation of a world where " everything is disturbed and out of its rightful place ". He feels too, however, that he has not given enough to God : " Everything perishes and I am spared." This is the reaction of the Christian who is too rich in the midst of poverty ; who is too happy when all around him suffer. In the ardour of his charity and faith he is at one with all those whom Christ redeemed. When he leaves for Jerusalem invisible companions walk beside him :

> " I am not alone ! A great concourse rejoices and sets out with me !
> The assembly of all my dead with me,
> And since it is true that the Christian is not alone but that he is in communion with all his brothers,
> It is the whole kingdom which with me calls to and draws towards the Seat of God and which resumes its straight course towards Him." (p.50).

.   .   .   .

To the many high moral qualities, to the living faith of this God-fearing man, the influence of dead Violaine later adds even greater detachment and resignation. The

43

troubled Christian, saddened by the disorder of the world, learns to abandon himself utterly to God in joy and peace.

For a few moments he evokes from the sunlight of a happy past the radiant child that had been Violaine ; apart from this however her death appears to leave him unnaturally calm. Jacques, shocked, blames this superficial indifference as well as Anne's exultation at the beauty, the richness of the earth at autumn, symbol of the fecundity of Grace. Only later, and then imperfectly, does Jacques understand the meaning of the peace by which the old man's soul is invaded. Jacques, even when he bows in submission, never knows the joy of a heart on fire with the love of God, of a soul borne up by the breath of the Holy Ghost.

Anne who earlier had been somewhat unjust with Mara is the first to beg Jacques to pardon her her crime and to forgive her himself. Humbly he realizes that his faith had been incomplete : exaggerated had been his worries about the destinies of dissension-torn France—Jeanne d'Arc's death had left her people free. Exaggerated especially had been his fears for the stability of the Church : God had not ceased to watch over all things and Anne sees Christendom conquer its difficulties and emerge from them stronger and more vital than ever. He had failed to perceive that, in spite of disorder and sorrow, in spite of the chaos of a world which had seemed close to disintegration, life continues and God remains as a force of unification. Already, on his return from the Holy Land the pilgrim had discerned in the night the symbol of salvation and of peace, " the morning star " which shines above the dark heights of Monsanvierge, " coming from Arabia " and now " over France, like a herald who rises up in the solitude " (p.181).

Henceforth his confidence is rather like that of the exquisite Dona Musica praying in the Church of St. Nicholas at Prague :

"What matters the disorder and the sorrow of to-day
     since it is the beginning of a new thing,
Since there is a morrow, since life goes on its way, using
     up with us the immeasurable reserves of creation,
Since the hand of God has not ceased moving and writ-
     ing with us on eternity, in lines short or long,
Down to the commas, down to the last perceptible
     full stop,
That book which will have no meaning until 'tis
     finished."[3]

Anne at last understands that God is ever-present, that He works secretly. Violaine had been wiser than he ; doubt and anxiety were unknown to her heart ; her childlike simplicity taught her the true meaning of prayer and sacrifice : it is not ordained that we must set forth on pilgrimages to distant lands ; God demands that, each in his appointed place, we continue our task in obedience and love. From Violaine, " the child of Grace " Anne has learned the true significance of detachment : suffering and death are accepted joyfully, for the Christian, however humble, however obscure, can co-operate in the Passion, in the Sacrifice of Calvary.

" God loves the joyful giver," says St. Paul to the Corinthians[4] and Anne echoes the spirit of his words :

" Is living the goal of life? shall the feet of the children of
     God be attached to this wretched earth?

[3] *The Satin Slipper*, p.135. (Sheed and Ward, 1931).
[4] IX, 7.

45

The question is not how we live but how we die, our
task is not to make the Cross but to mount on it and
to give smilingly all we have." (p.195).

He understands that, despite earthly separations, souls
remain united. The little dead girl is very close to the
living ; she continues her work of salvation. The light which
shines from her soul illumines those who remain and
makes bright the path which leads towards God :

" Walk in front, Violaine, my child, and I shall follow
you.

But sometimes turn your face towards me so that I may
see your eyes." (p.201).

This girl teaches him to accept with even greater resignation the solitude of old age and the approach of death. He
casts a last glance at the beauty of the earth, " green and
pink in spring, blue and blond in summer, brown or dead
white beneath the snow in winter." But from that too he
turns away. The old peasant, who all his days had loved the
golden sunlight gleaming on the burnished fields, walks
fearlessly towards the shadows, for his child leads him towards another radiance which is infinitely close and infinitely beautiful. The night through which he must pass is
necessary as a prelude to that eternal dawn. Nothing,
neither the death of those he loves nor the end of his life
task nor his solitude can impinge on his serenity :

" I live on the threshold of death and an inexpressible
joy is within me." (p.208).

CHAPTER VI.

VIOLAINE AND MARA

> " The sinner holds out his hand to
> the saint, gives his hand to the
> saint, since the saint gives his hand
> to the sinner. And both together,
> one through the other, they go up to
> Jesus."—*Un Nouveau Théologien* :
> *M. Fernand Laudet* by Charles Péguy.

THE redemption of Mara is a long and arduous task ; it
is not easy, however, to escape God. The most invulner-
able soul, the most avid for earthly possessions has, in its
armour, a weak point through which Grace can penetrate :
" If he goes not to You by what he has of light," says the
Jesuit praying for his brother, Rodrigue, " let him go to
You by what he has of darkness."[1] There was little enough
of light in Mara " the black " : her violence and jealousy
lead her to threats, to deceit and to crime ; her revolt
drives her to blasphemy. Yet, no more than the other
characters can she evade the light which radiates from
Violaine.

Mara, cruel and implacable as she is, is far from being an
exception in Claudel's theatre. He is too much of an
artist, a realist and a Christian, to ignore those souls "which
struggle in the chaos and the torments of dark mire ".[2]
Scenes, full of tragic intensity, show passions freed from all
restraint, in all their violence : ambition, hatred, vengeful
fury—brutal outbursts which most often lead to crime.

---

[1] *Satin Slipper*, p.3. (Sheed and Ward, 1931).
[2] *Conversations dans le Loir-et-Cher*, Dimanche. (Gallimard).

While it may be true that the evolution of Claudel's theatre tends to attenuate this primitive and savage violence, nevertheless in most of the plays we find a considerable number both of characters and situations almost barbaric in their cruelty: Avare (*La Ville*) rejoicing at the thought of destruction; Léchy Elbernon (*L'Echange*) setting fire to Thomas Pollock's house, then killing Louis Laine whom she loves; Ysé (*Partage de Midi*) unfaithful to her husband, abandoning her children, then leaving Mesa for Almaric, strangling her child and deserting Mesa, who is wounded, in a house which is about to be blown up; the Turelures, greedy, cunning and cruel: Toussaint, guilty of excesses during the Revolution; Louis, killing his father (*L'Otage*, *Le Pain dur*); Don Camille, the renegade, " with his false smile " (*Satin Slipper*).

In the two earlier versions of the play Mara[3] is already tenacious, harsh, wicked; a country girl who has one obsession: to conquer, to possess. She shrinks at nothing in order to attain her ends. Lies, insinuations about her sister, pressure brought to bear upon her mother, the threat to hang herself—all these weapons she employs in her effort to separate Jacques and Violaine. In the unfolding of the tragic conflict she it is who leads the action, who forces events. Less, however, than in the two earlier versions of *La jeune fille Violaine* where Mara is still more violent, still more cruel than in the *Tidings*. When Violaine, having signed an act of renunciation giving all her land to Bibiane, leaves Combernon, the latter, with a movement of scorn, throws a handful of ashes into her sister's eyes, blinding her.

[3] Her name, in the first version, is Bibiane. *Mara* in Hebrew means " bitter ". Cf. Book of Ruth, I, 20.

Her crime at the end is also more brutal : leading Violaine to a lonely spot she crushes her head on a stone[4]. Thus, in the *Tidings*, Claudel appears to have wished to attenuate the savage hardness of Mara ; nevertheless her detestation of her sister is no less violent. She hates Violaine : Violaine, the beautiful, the perfect, who is heiress to the best of their father's property and who, above all, is beloved by Jacques. Why should Violaine possess these graces, these privileges ; why are they not accorded to her who is destitute?

It can be admitted that Mara probably had some cause for her resentment. It would certainly be difficult for any ordinary mortal to live up to a sister such as Violaine, especially when, as Mara explains, " everything is for her and nothing for [Mara] " [p.55]. Even the fact that Violaine " always does what [Mara] wishes " (p.55) could do nothing to erase this resentment, for she cannot give to her sister the things which the latter desires : beauty, gentleness, the love of those around her. Mara is a very human, a too human figure, for if we understand her initial jealousy, all sympathy dies later when her hatred is relieved by no shade of pity. Mara has no word of compassion for her sister when, humanly speaking, Violaine has lost all : Jacques and Combernon, her beauty, her youth, her health ; when she is forced to live in utter solitude in the forest, feared by all, dependent on passers-by to throw her a few crusts of bread.

[4] Another example of the improvements which Claudel introduced into his final version : while theologically the Mara of the earlier version could have obtained pardon through repentance, it is doubtful whether it could be made esthetically satisfying. The murder is too brutal and crude in its details for an audience to pardon the woman responsible. The analogy of Regan and Goneril in *King Lear* immediately presents itself. Could even Shakespeare, after the scene with Gloucester, have made an audience believe in their redemption?

Like Mara, Sichel the proud, atheistic Jewess in *Le Pain dur*, struggles, revolts, defends herself both violently and bitterly: " I am a woman," cries Sichel, " and I wish to have my place with the rest of humanity; and for that I am ready to do all, to give all, to betray all."[5] Displaying the same tenacity as Mara, Sichel brings everything into play in order to entrap Louis Turelure, the son of her lover. She, like Mara, is not loved, but that matters little; what she wants is not merely the man but also his name and his future.

Mara, true peasant that she is, covets the land of Combernon but one thing counts above all: to win Jacques. This in her eyes makes all things permissible. She never hesitates, whether from moral scruples or purely human wisdom, before evildoing. Carried away, but nevertheless lucid, she scorns everything except her desired goal. And yet she is quite conscious of the fact that Jacques is not in love with her ; but nothing can alter her wild and desperate ardour. Violaine's love is grave, secret and pure ; that of Mara is " of another nature." It is passionate, obstinate, carnal :

" Blind, never letting go, like a deaf thing which does not hear.

In order that he possess me completely I had to possess him completely." (p.189).

Violaine renounces marriage but throughout her life and after her death she remains spiritually united to Jacques. She never defends herself, but this passivity springs not from a lack of love but from the fact that she has chosen God. Mara marries Jacques because she had sworn

[5] *Le Pain dur*, p.25. (Gallimard, 1918).

that he would be hers ; she would not " thus have let him go ". She remains however the girl who is neither beautiful nor pleasant, the girl who is not loved ; of this she is supremely aware :

" This love is not born of joy, it is born of sorrow ! This sorrow which suffices to those who have no joy." (p.190).

The death of her child leads to no spiritual awakening in her ; she is deeply moved but in a purely human sense. In an obscure, instinctive manner she does realize that Violaine's intervention is all-powerful with God. With a fierce obstinacy she demands a miracle for she has a peculiarly absolute confidence in her sister. For her, Violaine's holiness must serve earthly ends. Throughout that very tragic dialogue between the two sisters, in the calm of Christmas Eve, she remains bitter, ironical, rebellious against Heaven, scornful of the gentleness and trust in God of the recluse. She proudly proclaims herself to be of a different nature :

" Violaine, you know that I am hard-headed. I am she who never surrenders, who accepts nothing." (p.139).

But for Claudel each being, however guilty, is yet a soul which can be saved. In 1905 he wrote : " I know that, there where sin abounds, there Your Mercy abounds still more."[6] That is why God has already begun to work in that wounded heart. In the midst of her purely human sorrow she experiences a few instants of humility : while she reads the Christmas Office she suddenly feels herself to be unworthy of the beauty of the text. Her pride is somewhat shaken ; she regrets for an instant her harshness, her tenacity. When the

[6] *Corona Benignitatis Anni Dei*, p.119. (Gallimard).

child is restored to life, however, her passionate joy has in it nothing of the divine : she has not one word of thanks either for God or for Violaine. " Mara, the black " closes her heart to the supernatural. Soon her triumphant happiness at the resurrection of the child turns into jealousy and violence. Aubaine, her child, looks at her with the blue eyes of Violaine and Jacques' heart remains inaccessible to her. Whatever she may do, the shadow of Violaine will always stand between her and her husband ; although she is Jacques' wife her heart is torn by a hopeless love : " That is why ", she explains in the last Act, " I killed her in my despair."

In her intrigues, her ingratitude, her hard-heartedness, her jealous rage, her crime, Mara shows the same obstinacy which she displays in all things. How slowly she repents ; one is almost tempted to ask sometimes, does she repent? She admits her hatred, her crime ; she tries to justify it, hiding nothing ; her challenge is not without dignity :

" Is it my fault if I loved Jacques? Was it for my joy or in order that my soul might be consumed by flames? What could I do to defend myself, I who am neither beautiful nor attractive ; I, poor woman, who can give only sorrow? " (p.190).

With a pathetic lucidity she sees herself, she judges herself : a creature bereft of light and grace, incapable of exciting love, dry and hard ; completely deficient in the wonderful beauty of soul which Violaine had possessed. She compares herself to her sister :

" Nobody takes pleasure in seeing her [Mara], ah, it is not the flower in its season,

52

But that which lies beneath withering flowers, the earth itself, the miserly earth beneath the grass, the earth of which there is never any lack." (pp.190-1).

In the depths of her heart there had certainly existed a capacity for generosity and kindness ; happy love could have brought this to fruition. In other circumstances she might have been an excellent wife, a woman rather hard and grasping, but nevertheless respected by all. But because, largely through her own fault, she is rejected by those closest to her, she finds in her moral solitude fresh food for her bitterness and anger.

Her hatred, like everything else she attempts, ends in failure. Violaine's death is but a " poor, unskilful crime ", powerless to obtain for her what she desires. True, she possesses Combernon, she has Jacques and her daughter. But does this give her the happiness of which she had dreamed? For now she knows that she will for ever remain " she who is not loved and for whom nothing succeeds " (p.190). She begins to realize that she had striven by human means to overcome that which was wholly spiritual.

Her character is somewhat redeemed by her despairing love and by the brutal honesty which she displays even in evil : " I have committed a great crime, I have killed my sister, but against you I have not sinned " (p.191) she cries out to Jacques in her pride-filled confession. At that moment however, while she faces God we feel that she is still defiant and obstinate in her sin. Nevertheless, God's grace is stronger and dead Violaine draws this rebellious soul towards her.

In his recent speech at the reception of Claudel in the French Academy, François Mauriac, analysing *Partage de Midi*, stressed the mysterious and diverse paths which Grace follows : " God is there in the heart of Mesa to save him . . . not in spite of his sin but . . . I am almost tempted to say, because of his sin."[7] While it is true that the hard peasant, Mara, is far from possessing the burning, passionate heart of Mesa, nevertheless the position is similar. Mara's crime was so great that it left her vulnerable, overwhelmed with a sense of guilt. An emotion near akin to remorse at last rends her :

"O Jacques, I am no longer the same! Something in me is finished !

Something in me is broken ! " (p.192).

Patiently God has laid his snares for this stormy soul. The *etiam peccata* of St. Augustine, which strikes the key-note of the *Satin Slipper*, applies equally to Mara : Sin also serves to save. The gravity of her crime helps to crush her pride ; its failure allows Grace to penetrate her. Then, through Violaine's death, she is, despite herself, led with the others, though far behind them, up the ascent which mounts towards God. She experiences peace, a peace which brings but little joy : the peace of being pardoned, of accepting life with its monotonous duties, its obscure tasks. She is still the woman who is not loved ; perhaps, indeed, it is through that human humiliation, through the loss of all terrestial hope, that she will eventually learn to turn completely towards God and the things of the spirit.

[7] Speech of François Mauriac, 12th March, 1947.

CHAPTER VII.

VIOLAINE AND JACQUES HURY

> " There is no barrier impassible to
> the Grace of God."—*Introduction à
> un poème sur Dante.*

TO lead Anne Vercors, already a just man, closer to the
supernatural ; to snatch from sin Pierre, the poet-
architect ; to conquer Mara, an upright soul even in her
brutality and hatred—all this was infinitely simpler than to
save Jacques Hury from his mediocrity. He is only " a rough
and simple man ", a " wingless man ", so close to earth
that for a long time Heaven appears inaccessible to him.
His is not an ardent soul capable of sudden, irremediable
falls ; he is completely without metaphysical disquiet.
" A Christian soul can be made from a pagan soul," wrote
Charles Péguy, " but what shall we do with those which are
nothing . . . . neither spiritual nor carnal, neither pagan
nor Christian, those living dead? "[1]

In the beginning of the play Jacques appears as a shrewd
peasant ; full of self-confidence, hard towards the poor,
somewhat scornful of Anne Vercors to whom he owes everything. He is ready to do his duty towards Monsanvierge,
to fill with food the basket lowered by the recluses each
morning ; but he must not be expected to understand the
meaning of the contemplative life : " Heaven for the
heavenly and earth for the earthly." (p.91).

It is true that he loves in Violaine her freshness, her youth
and her gentleness ; yet soon we ask ourselves to what extent,

[1] *Clio*, Oeuvres Completes, viii. p.253. (Gallimard, 1917).

unconsciously perhaps, he is influenced by the thought of the possessions which will be his as a result of this marriage. He states frankly that he was given both Monsanvierge and the young girl because " that was just ". To which Violaine replies :

" But I, Jacques, I do not love you because that is just . . .
There can be no question of justice between us." (p.91).

The separation between these two beings has already begun.

If the betrothal scene—so intensely dramatic—opens in the light and joy of love, it ends in the bitter sorrow of loneliness. Their beautiful and fragile happiness fades before the certainty that no true communion is possible between these two souls. They have chosen different paths. Jacques' fine words of love at their engagement stress only too cruelly his harshness, his violence, his reproaches, his complete lack of pity when he learns that Violaine is now a leper. Her protestations of her innocence do not touch him. He is blinded by anger and he answers her only by a furious accumulation of insults :

" Damned wretch,
Damned in your soul and in your flesh." (p.98).

She is judged and condemned without even being heard. His reaction is to get her away as soon as possible. For, he says, " We must avoid scandal " and, as well, he fears the contagious nature of leprosy. We know, instinctively, how different would have been Pierre de Craon's attitude in similar circumstances.

The flaw which might be found in the *Tidings* lies here. How could Violaine love this rough, ordinary, prosaic being? How can Jacques who is egoistical and vain, sing in such splendid words all the exultation of young love, all its moving tenderness? Prostrate before the face of happiness he cries:

" O my betrothed through the flowering branches, . . .
　How beautiful you are Violaine! and how beautiful
　　is the world where you are.
　This share which was reserved to me . . .
　Violaine how lonely is this place and how private it is
　　here with you!" (pp.82-3-4).

His soul is touched. Violaine's poignant loveliness transforms and invades for a moment the arid solitude of this man's life. The hymn owes its origin much less to carnal love than to the fact that a mysterious sweetness possesses his whole being. For once we feel in Jacques the disquiet which must inevitably arise when, conscious of the finiteness, the instability inherent in all we perceive, we catch a glimpse of absolute beauty. Nevertheless, the problem remains: how can the mediocrity of Jacques be reconciled with so much poetic emotion? Elsewhere indeed Claudel says: " Who will dare to state that love is clear? "[2] It is true that certain affections remain mysterious and inexplicable, yet we understand Mara's passion for Jacques; that of Sygne for Georges; that of Prouhèze for the independent and obstinate Rodrigue. But how far removed is Jacques from Violaine! The only possible solution appears to be that Claudel desired to show that Violaine could awaken in him a fine and poignant emotion utterly foreign to his nature; that God, through Grace, could transform him.

For God will utilize Jacques' love in order that He may

[2] *Toi, qui es-tu?* p.51. (Gallimard, 3rd ed.).

penetrate into this somewhat gross soul, steeped in earthly desires, separated from spiritual realities. To ensure that so much mediocrity be stirred, that the hidden chink be discovered in the armour, Jacques has to experience the humiliation of believing Violaine guilty, the suffering of losing her and the additional pain which, we can guess, results from his marriage to Mara. Perhaps this love, less ardent, less spiritual than that of Rodrigue in the *Satin Slipper*, is the answer to a prayer something like that which the Jesuit, dying on the open sea, addresses to God for his brother :

" Clog him by the weight of this other lovely being which lacks him and is calling to him across the space between

Make him a wounded man apart, for that once in his life he has seen the face of an angel ! "[3]

Contrasted with Jacques' love, that of Violaine appears in all its beauty. What she seeks is not that which can escape her—the perishable—but the spiritual being. For her, love implies the acceptance of a great responsibility : a soul is entrusted to her as if it were a precious treasure ; the beloved being is something eternal and infinite. It is for this reason that she understands Jacques' mediocrity so quickly, love, as he conceives it, is limited to the earth and she knows that the only thing which she has to offer, her soul in all its purity, will be rejected :

" What would Jacques have done with the only thing which I could have given him? " (p.135)

she asks herself later on.

[3] *Satin Slipper*, p.3. (Sheed and Ward, 1931).

She has, in the scene in the garden, although doubts well up, a confidence in Jacques, a belief that, although marriage in the ordinary sense is impossible, her betrothed will consent to a spiritual union. That is why she comes to him dressed in the dalmatic which the women of Combernon wore twice in their lives: when they became engaged and at their death[4]. In her youth and innocence she sees no impossibility inherent in such a union. Her own love, although it does not find expression in passionate words as does that of Prouhèze, is ardent beneath all her gentleness. Through long years of suffering she will remain faithful to the man who cast her aside. Neither was she without bitterness at the thought that visited her after she had contracted leprosy: that Jacques might abandon her. When she was told of Mara's threat to commit suicide if the marriage took place she had laughed but, says Elizabeth, " It is not the laugh which I like from my little girl" (p.75). Were it not that we feel this undercurrent of passion Violaine would be too much " milk and honey ", too gentle, too self-effacing. The child-like faith, which sometimes stills her doubts, makes her infinitely touching. Pathetically she believes that he can save her: " Will you not be able to preserve your little one who loves you? " (p.87) and later again, " Who knows if you will not be well able to defend and preserve me? " (p.87). The words of the dying girl seems to stress this faith: by love she might have been saved:

" If you had believed in me
Who knows but you might have cured me." (p.163.)

---

[4] The dalmatic would seem to symbolize here her earthly love, her divine love and, finally, her death to the world.

Because she is human she tries, if only for a short time, to make Jacques repeat to her gentle words of love ; she strives to prolong the joy of the present, to forget her leprosy :

" Don't say anything to me. I don't ask you anything.
      You are there and that is enough for me . . .
      Ah ! how beautiful is this hour. I don't ask for any
      other." (p.84).

But already she knows, in her innermost soul, that her pleas are vain, that her union with Jacques will never be on this earth. Nevertheless this child, for she is no more, crushed under the weight of her secret, terrified by the thought of the future, utters in this light-flooded garden a cry of anguish and fear ; a pathetic and trusting call to the man who, a few minutes later, repels her harshly :

" Oh, take your little one with you, let her be found no
      more and let nobody harm her." (p.85).

Her hope dies and the impression of solitude overwhelms her. Once again, for the last time, she immobilizes the present ; no longer in order to taste a sweetness that she knows to be illusionary, but so that Jacques may preserve the memory of this exceptional moment :

" Am I not beautiful enough in this instant, Jacques?
      What more do you ask of me?
      What does one ask of a flower
      Except that it be beautiful and fragrant for an instant,
      poor flower, and afterwards it will be the end." (p.92).

Already she contrasts this human happiness with spiritual love. Not without sorrow has she torn herself away from earthly joy ; she has begun her abnegation and sacrifice. If in tragic and bitter words she offers Jacques the only union which remains possible between them she feels now, and it is this knowledge which tortures her, that she will be met by incomprehension and refusal:

" Is my soul not enough? Take it and I am still here and
    assimilate it, even to its profoundest depths, that
    which is yours!

.   .   .   .   .

What more would you do with me? fly, go far away!
    Why do you want to marry me? Why do you desire
To take for yourself that which belongs to God alone?
The hand of God is upon me and you cannot defend
    me!" (pp.92-3).

Already she submits herself utterly to the demands of God. That partly explains why she makes so little effort to defend herself, she who is so pure, when she is falsely accused. She could doubtless protect herself somewhat by accusing Mara, but she knows already that Jacques will marry her sister. In any case it would be of no avail, her rupture with Jacques was already consummated; her pleading would be vain. At this moment when her human love is mortally wounded, divine love triumphs. If she lets fall a few words of bitter irony, if her attitude towards Jacques is somewhat scornful, she ceases to struggle. It is not weakness which causes her to permit Jacques to believe her guilty; moral strength makes her realize that it is her vocation to go towards God in suffering and solitude. Moreover, Jacques' love could never have satisfied this heart which craved to be filled to overflowing. Like Mesa in *Partage de Midi* Violaine could have cried:

61

" Ah ! you are not happiness, you are that which is in the
place of happiness ! "[5]

What she sought when she came, clad in the golden dalmatic of the nuns of Monsanvierge, into this flower-filled
garden was not so much a few tender words of love as
something infinite and immortal.

Her realization of the fragility of all human affections,
Mara's treachery, her mother's weakness, Jacques' mediocrity, her leprosy—that sign of God's will—all these combine
and explain her calm decision to go forth alone. In her
sacrifice there is none of the violence of Sygne who, in
L'Otage, tears herself away from Georges' love only after
an atrocious struggle and casts herself, almost despairing,
into God's arms. Violaine, " gentle Violaine ", understands
quickly and absolutely the meaning of her strange vocation.
Her father, on his return after her death, shows that he fully
comprehends this aspect of her character :

" Why torture oneself when it is simple to obey?
Thus does Violaine immediately, promptly, follow the
hand which takes hers." (p.196).

She leaves behind her her happy childhood, the fair land of
Combernon, her family and her love. Simply, silently she
begins her walk down that long, lonely path that leads to
death. She too could say :

" Things abandon me little by little, and I, I in my turn,
abandon them.

---

[5] Cf. see also *Cantate à trois Voix*, p.22. (Gallimard, 1943).
" Happiness
Belongs to this very hour
When he whom our heart loves is absent."

Only denuded of all things can one enter into the secrets of love."[6]

After she has experienced eight years of pain and seclusion we come on Violaine again. Blind, worn away by leprosy, she has not ceased to love Jacques but her love has become more and more spiritualized :

" The soul alone survives in that perished body," (p.129) and it is her soul alone which is united to Jacques. When, dying, she is borne back to Combernon she finds the same rough, self-centred man, full of self-pity. Inconsequent, like all weak individuals, he has forgotten the haste with which he sent Violaine to the cave of Géyn. In his eyes circumstances, together with Violaine's generosity and sacrifice, are alone responsible for their separation. He reminds us of the second category of beings which Pascal describes : " There are only two sorts of men : on one hand, the just who believe themselves sinners ; on the other, sinners who believe themselves just."[7] For Jacques does not seem to take any blame for himself. Violaine, faced by so much self-assurance, rediscovers something of the slightly mocking tone of the happy young girl of the Prologue. Patiently and indulgently ironical she answers his complaints about his misfortunes :

" Poor boy !
And I, have I not suffered a little ? " (p.161).

She recalls to his mind his past complacency :

" And tell me, what is Justice's share in all that? that Justice of which you used to speak so proudly? " (p.166).

---

[6] La Messe là-bas, p.13. (Gallimard, 1919).
[7] Pensées, xiii, p.423. (éd. Brunschvigg).

or again :

"Poor fellow, you know nothing at all about women."
(p.174).

For the last time she strains every nerve to convince this obtuse intelligence, to move this earth-bound spirit, to touch this man in his innermost being.

During this parting scene she tells Jacques how she met her fatal accident. He had appeared to pay little attention to Pierre's account of his discovery of the leper girl. In answer to Jacques' assurance that deliverance from her suffering is at hand, Violaine makes an unexpected statement which awakens the man's suspicions :

"Violaine : Blessed then be the hand which guided me
     the other night.

Jacques : What hand?

Violaine : That hand which, as I returned from my
     search for food,
     Silently grasped mine and guided me

Jacques : Where to?

Violaine : To where Pierre de Craon found me,
     Under a great sand heap, a whole cart load
     upset on top of me. Did I get there by my-
     self? " (p.167).

At a first reading this revelation seems inartistic and inconsistent. We should have expected Violaine to maintain her heroic reticence to the end. For earlier had she not unprotestingly accepted her abandonment by Jacques? Certainly we cannot imagine that now, at the end, she seeks revenge. M. J. Madaule believes that this revelation may have been deliberately made in order that Jacques' life will be henceforth based on reality not on illusion :

"Just as he now knows everything about Violaine, so he must be aware of everything which concerns Mara, of her jealous love which refuses to release its hold and of the dark depths of her criminal soul." [7a]

Even this interpretation presents certain difficulties. If Violaine deliberately and lucidly decided that for the sake of Jacques' ultimate happiness she was bound to speak, how explain her attitude when, after her initial statement which we quoted, she does all in her power to avoid answering Jacques' indignant questions? For a short time she in fact succeeds in changing the subject of conversation.

Is it not possible that at the thought of the welcome approach of death, she unconsciously spoke aloud her prayer—a prayer of forgiveness—and, assuming that Jacques knew the circumstances of her discovery by Pierre, asks impatiently : " Did I get there by myself? " Then realizing what she has done she vainly endeavours to repair her slip.

Later, faced by Jacques' obstinacy and by his sure instinct which tells him the name of the criminal, she decides that the whole question must be faced, discussed and dismissed once and for all.

Perhaps too, as M. Madaule thinks, she realizes slowly that such an explanation is even desirable. If Jacques, casting aside his egoism, seeks the spiritual, it will be henceforth in the naked brutal light of truth. He will accept Mara as she is, with her crime but also with her desperate ardent love for him. Is he not responsible for his wife's

[7a] *Le Drame de Paul Claudel*, p.252.

soul, for her salvation? For this reason Violaine's last gift
to Jacques is the statement that renunciation and sacrifice
are essential to him:

". . . you must have a clearly marked duty.
That is why my hair is full of sand." (p. 175).

Thus the strange and disconcerting revelation was
necessary. Violaine's terrible demands on Jacques may be
only the result of foresight and common sense. Had she
died silently, discretely, could she have prevented Jacques'
life from being poisoned by suspicions? Sooner or later this
slow, obstinate man would have sought and found the cause
of her death and she would no longer have been there to
teach him resignation and mercy. For if, dying, she calls
on Jacques to face a difficult, sorrowful life, her insistence
that he pardon Mara is no less forceful. She shows him his
duty: he must cultivate the land of Combernon. He will
not be alone; he has his daughter, whom she has restored
to him; he has Mara who knows and loves him, who is of
Violaine's own blood. That is his vocation; the fact that it
is dull and joyless is of no moment; does she not tell him:
" You were not promised happiness." (p. 175)

Jacques, overcome at finding his former betrothed not
guilty as he had imagined but ever faithful to him, cannot
bring himself to believe that their separation is now inevitable, that they can know no happiness on earth. Violaine,
on the contrary, realizes the danger which a total and
absolute human love can be to the soul which seeks God:
" It was too beautiful and we should have been too happy."
And elsewhere Claudel makes one of his characters say:
" To love him apart from God means an insufficient

love."[8] For Violaine, however, there remains the wonderful possibility of a spiritual and eternal union.

Here we touch on one of Claudel's favourite themes: sacrifice is better than possession: " Human love is beautiful only when it is unsatisfied."[9] And in *Le Père humilié* we find the same idea expressed:

" It is necessary that I should not be a happy man, it is necessary that I should not be a satisfied man !

It is necessary that my mouth and eyes should not be clogged with that sort of happiness which removes desire from us."[10]

Carnal love ends often only in defeat and despair. That is why love, in most of Claudel's plays, is thwarted and unhappy. Here Jacques marries not Violaine but Mara ; in *L'Otage* Sygne weds not Georges but Turelure ; little Countess Lumîr in *Le Pain dur* returns alone to Poland and Louis Turelure is united to the Jewess, Sichel, whom he despises ; in *Le Père humilié* Pensée marries not Orian whom she loves but his brother ; in the *Satin Slipper* Prouhèze is the wife of Camille not of Rodrigue. Prouhèze, however, remains eternally united to him from whom she is eternally separated even though she knows full well that her love, from an earthly point of view, can never be satisfied : " And I ", says Rodrigue at the end, " I only held her beautiful hand for a moment against my cheek."[11]

This curious conception of love sometimes makes us think of Corneille although the heroes of the *Cid* and of *Polyeucte*

[8] *L'Otage*, p.131. (Gallimard, 22nd ed.).
[9] *Correspondance avec Jacques Rivière*, p.262. (Plon-Nourrit, 1926).
[10] *Le Père Humilié*, pp.131-2. (Gallimard, 6th ed.).
[11] *Satin Slipper*, Fourth Day, Sc. XI. (Sheed and Ward, 1931)

experience in their victorious renunciation an exultation unknown to those of Claudel's plays. The characters created by the modern poet tear themselves away with difficulty from their earthly attachments. It is essential to realize that in Claudel's theatre it is not always forbidden passions which are in question—passions which could be satisfied only by sin. This is indeed the case in *Partage de Midi*, *L'Echange* and in the greater part of the *Satin Slipper*. In *L'Otage*, however, Sygne is, from a human point of view, perfectly free to marry Georges. In the *Tidings* no moral issue prevents Violaine from being the wife of Jacques. This does not mean that Claudel disbelieves in the vocation of marriage ; on the contrary he has a very high conception of its dignity. Ceaselessly Marthe in *L'Echange* recalls it to Louis Laine :

" And consider my soul, and I, wonderingly, shall take yours with veneration

In my arms, having cast myself on my knees, since it is the creation of God

And His sacred trust against my heart, between my arms."[12]

In the same way the Pope in *Le Père humilié* stresses to his nephews the profound meaning of the Sacrament :

" But marriage is not pleasure, it is the sacrifice of pleasure, it is the study of two souls which henceforth, for ever,

Will have to content themselves one with the other."[13]

But while Claudel certainly does not reject marriage[14]

---

[12] *Théâtre*, iii. p.223-4. (Mercure de France).
[13] p.107. (Gallimard, 6th ed.).
[14] Cf. also, " Letters on Coventry Patmore " in *Positions et Propositions*, i, pp.30-2. (Gallimard).

it remains true, as M. André Molitor wisely remarked, that " sin and heroic spiritual love following renunciation are more familiar to his work ".[15] In these plays where heroism predominates, that which is human must be sacrificed to a higher order.

Thus, those who are torn apart, frustrated, may, by a marvellous compensation, be united in spirit and of this they are often conscious. So Prouhèze, ardent and passionate, aspiring desperately to be " that laughing, sobbing bride in his arms " accepts separation that she may be instead " this eternal star for which he thirsts ", a light guiding him towards God. Prouhèze achieves that superhuman attitude only after a long struggle. Violaine, less passionate and apparently more detached, Violaine the dying leper, voices brief but poignant regrets. She remembers the time of her engagement : " How hard it is to renounce when the heart is young " ; or, calling to mind the glory of the harvest fields at Combernon, she cries suddenly : " How fine it is to live ! " But her weariness is extreme and her desire for God is more powerful ; the thought of death is sweet to the woman who has tasted all sorrows :

" . . . it is good too to die ! Then, when it is well ended
      and when, little by little, over us is spread
   The darkening as of a very dark shade." (pp.177-8).

And, in spite of the regrets which make her so genuine and so human, at the very moment of her supreme sacrifice, she does not forget Jacques. When he laments her loss she contrasts the beauty, the eternity of their spiritual union to the precariousness of earthly love. Of what importance is it, Claudel's characters seem to say, if beings, created to love

[15] *Aspects de Paul Claudel*, p.148. (Desclée De Brouwer, 1945).

each other, are severed from that love on earth, since all that human sorrow merely serves to prepare the meeting which knows no separation in another world : " When earth does but uproot you, it's in the sky that you will take root again,"[16] says Saint James meditating on the strange destiny of Prouhèze and Rodrigue. It is because she is possessed by this inviolable certitude that Violaine patiently explains to Jacques the meaning of life : it consists in suffering, but in suffering lucidly—and the meaning of death : a liberation from the body, that envelope which conceals the secrets of the heart. Her own death is not even a separation : " I remain, I do not go away " (p.169). The union between their souls will be closer than ever in " the communion on the Cross ". Little by little she forces the egoistic man to abandon self. The " just man " now agrees that he lacks something, he is less sure of himself ; that, doubtless, is all that God, for the moment, requires of him. He blames himself, he humiliates himself, he at last weeps at the thought of the eight years of solitude and suffering which the leper girl has experienced. And we feel that he is ready to accept both the death of Violaine and the prospect of life with Mara. It is true that still, in Act IV, he has instants of revolt and of despair at the thought of his loss, for now only, at this moment of separation, has he realized Violaine's full worth. Yet he, too, progresses towards peace. After Mara's confession he pardons her in Violaine's name ; he takes her back because of Violaine. He, the avaricious peasant proud of owning Combernon, offers to return the land to Anne Vercors. He accuses himself, before them all, of having doubted Violaine. His resignation is slow but real : " It is

[16] *Satin Slipper*, p.98. (Sheed and Ward, 1931).

well thus, it is well thus," he repeats with effort at the end of the play. His lumbering, limited intelligence has doubtless failed to grasp fully the meaning, the beauty of Violaine's sacrifice, the extent of her spiritual richness, but already, by a mysterious attachment of his heart, he is led towards supernatural regions.

His peace is attained only with difficulty and, compared with that of Anne and Pierre, it is joyless. As with Mara, it lies only in the acceptance of a humble life and the feeling of duty done. In the purely spiritual domain he will always move only by a tremendous effort. His walk along that path will be clumsy, heavy—that of a cripple, leaning on the frail shoulder of a young girl who patiently guides him towards God up the only way which he can tread, slowly, without exultation, without mystical fervour.

CHAPTER VIII.

VIOLAINE'S SACRIFICE

> "I give them tryst upon a lake of gold."—*Satin Slipper*.

IN the gilded light of a late afternoon in Autumn the characters, freed from their passions, their worries, their discord, all led by dead Violaine, attain, doubtless in different ways, but genuinely and truly, to peace. Grace has visited them. The whole play is a progression towards God, towards joy—that joy, incomprehensible to unbelievers, which is for Christians " a horrible, an absurd, a poignant reality ".[1]

In the heart of the drama stands a little girl, simple, angelic, somewhat silent ; one who does not analyse herself very much : Violaine, the beautiful, the beloved, the happy, who becomes Violaine the leper, the lonely, the blind ; Violaine, laughing, spontaneous, joyful who, through sorrow, solitude, sacrifice and prayer becomes a detached, spiritualized being ; this very human child who, in the midst of gladness, knowing herself to be loved, cries with a truly Pascalian note : " Ah, how big the world is and how alone we are in it." (p.88). And, while she walks the path of utter abnegation, she preserves, despite her mystical ardour, illusions, fears and regrets.

The wound caused by a great human love was necessary in order that she might understand the bitter fact that souls are incommunicable ; that she might realize the emptiness

---

[1] *Le Père humilié*, p.118. (Gallimard, 6th ed.).

of that affection whichcannot satisfy the hunger of the heart ; that she might fear as illusionary and precarious, joys that were too purely terrestrial. Deliberately, promptly she chose the sorrows of separation. Like Prouhèze she understands that " there is nothing for which man is so unfitted as happiness, nothing of which he sickens so soon."[2]

That is why Violaine chose God and became, through her bodily and spiritual sacrifices, a living victim : " The male is the priest but it is not forbidden to the woman to be a victim " (p.135) she says to Mara on that strange Christmas Eve. Her vocation is one of sacrifice. She belongs to that race of very pure beings who, with a gesture of sublime folly, are capable of breaking all earthly bonds : " Great and unheard of things, our heart is such that it cannot resist them,"[3] says Sygne. Not only did Violaine renounce all earthly happiness but she took upon herself the task of expiating the sin of Pierre de Craon ; she contracted the leprosy of which he was miraculously healed—leprosy symbolic of the fault of which she has offered to bear the weight. She accepts the humiliation of being abandoned by Jacques whom she has not ceased to love, of being hated by Mara, of being driven away into the solitude of the forest amidst the scorn of all. The blind girl in *La jeune fille Violaine* was venerated by the people, the poor flocked to her. Here the leper, " the faceless one ", is brutally treated by those who surround her ; from time to time they disdainfully throw her a crust of dry bread. Alone she faces the physical torture of a slow and terrible death. She has chosen sorrow which consumes every impurity : "Happy is he who suffers and who knows why." (p.165). In order that Vio-

[2] *Satin Slipper*, First Day, Scene 10. (Sheed and Ward, 1931).
[3] *L'Otage*, p.169. (Gallimard, 22th ed.).

laine may accomplish her destiny she must continue to live, she must have time to become that flower of holiness which grows slowly in the dark cave of Géyn. A quick death would have been too simple. As with Beata in the *Cantate à trois Voix*, exile is wearily prolonged in order that the bloom may have attained to the splendour of its maturity before God plucks it:

> " Oh, let him remain somewhat in the distance ! I desire this, that still, for a little space, he should remain in the distance !
>
> Since what of faith if he were here? what of time? what of desire? and how could one become fully, if he were there, a rose?
>
> It is his absence alone which gives birth to us."[4]

Claudel merely implies and suggests the sufferings of the eight years during which Violaine's life is veiled in shadows and she listens to " things existing with [her] ", studying herself ; alone, but alone with God Who is present with her " as with all who suffer " (p.131). A few sentences from her conversation with Mara, completely without bitterness though she is, permit us to guess the intensity of her slow agony. She has experienced all the misery of knowing that her physical pain will last as long as her body lives[5] ; she has

---

[4] p.25. (Gallimard, 1943). Cf. also *Magnificat* :
" He who participates in the Will of God must participate also in His silence.

Be with Me absolutely. Let us be silent together before all.

He who gives life must accept death."

[5] It is curious to compare Violaine's words on the spiritual significance of suffering to that other poem which Claudel published in *La Vie intellectuelle*, 10th April, 1938, from which the following lines are extracted. The title is " To the lepers of Hôpital St. Louis :

struggled wearily in the long monotony of solitary days, made but more desolate by the memory of her happy childhood. All have abandoned her and she bends beneath the weight of these souls to which she is linked. That is not stressed, however ; her complaints are restrained, brief. Perhaps this is one of the reasons why Violaine appears almost too suave ; why we occasionally get the impression of a too facile perfection. She is indeed by nature, like Marthe in *L'Echange*, tender, submissive, forgetful of self. To this race of beings one may prefer Ysé, laughing, passionate, troubled, or especially the complex personality of Prouhèze, more mischievous, more vivacious, prouder and more capable of revolt yet no less ready to surrender, after a pathetically intense struggle, to God. If, however,

---

How do you come, Grace of God?
She says : With fresh water !
A big bunch of fresh roses !
All the house is on fire !
But you, my child, be not afraid !
He whom I hold in my arms,
He is there and I am there.
It is I, I am the Lord.

You suffer, my child, you weep !
And I, I kiss your heart !
Hear this strange word :
To-morrow you will be an angel !

So much the worse for this poor house
If I have destroyed it a bit !
This God with you, this Brother,
You haven't paid too dearly for Him.
I am fire ! He who touches Me
Must consent to be burnt.
A victim, a living sacrifice,
Do you cease to be My child?
My child, My only child !
And if I took your tunic from you
Of what use was that vesture?

75

Violaine appears to fulfil her destiny almost without effort, or at least without a too violent spiritual torment, is this not essentially due to the fact that her heroism is merely suggested? We are left to reconstruct a little too much for ourselves her struggles against her own desires, against her fear of loneliness, against her horror of that living death. We do not see clearly enough the slow formation of her holiness amidst the shadows of that cave where she passes eight long and atrocious years. At the end of that period, when we rediscover her, she is calm, freed from all temptation, totally given over to God, filled with the meaning of her strange vocation. She knows that " the Son of man has come not to destroy suffering but to suffer with us ".[6] In answer to His appeal she had set out to follow Him, never glancing back, walking steadily towards the Cross which dominates the play; it is on Calvary that the soul is most intimately united to Jesus. There and there only is it possible for us to " adapt ourselves and to become absolutely at one with the Lamb Who here is engaged in dying our death."[7]

Thus often in Claudel's plays does one woman profoundly influence those who come into contact with her. Her mission is to overwhelm man and to give him a thirst for infinity. " I am the promise which cannot be kept," says Lala in La Ville[8], " and my grace consists in that very fact ; I am the sweetness of what is, combined with the regret of what is not ". Marthe, in L'Echange, cannot save Louis Laine, her husband, but she does give a chance of salvation to the other characters. In the Satin Slipper, Prouhèze,

[6] Toi qui es-tu? p.113. (Gallimard, 3rd ed.).
[7] L'Epée et le Miroir, p.85. (Gallimard, 1939).
[8] Théâtre, ii, p.307. (Mercure de France, 1929).

separated from Rodrigue, casts him towards God. Thus woman, who can be a source of sin, becomes most often a means of salvation. Great is the number of woman characters who are in different ways, images and symbols of Grace.

But if the sacrifice demanded appears cruel, even inhuman, it is not vain. Violaine, through her free gift of herself, through her acceptance of bodily death, through the mysterious union of divine Grace with so much humiliation and human misery, attains to a strangely sweet spiritual happiness. She has understood that which Orian tries to explain to Pensée :

" Pensée : The Cross is suffering.
Orian : It is redemption.
Pensée : We don't want suffering.
Orian : Who then will kill in you that which is capable of dying?
Pensée : We don't want suffering.
Orian : Therefore you do not want joy."[9]

For through this sorrow sacrifice is enfolded in a great joy : " For according as the sufferings of Christ abound in us, so through Christ doth our comfort also abound."[10] As peace wells into her tortured body Violaine tastes a happiness which is already heavenly. In the same way that Christ was incarnate through Mary's " Fiat " so, through Violaine's resignation, is spiritual life born again :

" Thus the man who suffers is not useless and idle !
He works and merits, by his collaboration with the kindly and cruel hand which is acting upon him, not

[9] *Le Père humilié*, p.70. (Gallimard, 6th ed.).
[10] II. Cor. i. 5.

77

perishable and relative goods but absolute values of which he has the deposition."[11]

Without pride Violaine realizes that she can act as an instrument in the saving of a divided world which is troubled by a thousand passions and spiritually impoverished. Thus she attributes to her sacrifice a social sense:

" That is why my body is in labour in place of Christendom which is falling apart . . .

Powerful is suffering when it is as voluntary as sin." (p.136).

This " child of Grace " provides God with a means of touching the hearts of those who surround her. The *Tidings* is the drama of the ascension of this soul towards death and towards eternity: a difficult progression, for Violaine leads with her a whole group of beloved ones whom she raises or saves. In Claudel's own words, we assist here at a scene where we behold " weak creatures in combat with Grace ". They resist, defend themselves or slowly permit themselves to be vanquished, but all are struck in their innermost being.

Violaine's death, " death, our very precious patrimony ",[12] completes her work of sacrifice. When she enters into eternal life she leaves in the hearts of all a great sweetness, an ineffable peace: " Death has lost its meaning."[13] Violaine is absent but the light which shines from her soul remains with those who must live on and they are all in varying degrees, according to their collaboration with Grace, less earthy, more detached, closer to God.

Through Violaine a certain disorder has been eliminated.

[11] *Toi qui es-tu?* p.113. (Gallimard, 3rd ed.).
[12] *Art Poétique*, p.156. (Mercure de France, 1913).
[13] *Tête d'or*, Th. i. p.386. (Mercure de France).

The object of Claudel's works is to restore to a world contaminated by original sin a little of its lost harmony. In a letter to Gabriel Frizeau, written when he was composing his first plays, Claudel already stated his aim: to show " the desperate effort of a soul which cannot resign itself to the fact of not finding, in this visible world which surrounds it the order, the peace and the joy of which it possesses a strong and sure knowledge."[14]

> " All the characters of his plays ", writes Jacques Madaule, " seek passionately that place of which they will at last have the right to say that it is theirs and that it is where God has sent them. For each of us this correct place exists, and it is our very vocation to reach it, to recognize it and to stay there . . . Tribulations, failure, pain and sometimes death serve that end."[15]

Anne, Pierre, Jacques and Mara now each follows his own path. They accept their life, the place which is accorded to them, they are faithful to themselves and to the part which they must play. In death Violaine is not separated from them, she continues her work of expiation: " Our occupation for eternity ", writes Claudel, " will be . . . the maintenance of our equilibrium in an immense, loving, perfect communion of all our brothers, the elevation of our voice in the indescribable moan of Love."[16]

At the end in the calm of evening, when
> " The wains which pass along the road
> Leave wisps of straw on boughs loaded with fruit "
> (p.183),

and when the silence is made vibrant by the hammer

[14] *Revue intellectuelle*, xxxvii (1935). p.36.
[15] *Le Drame de Paul Claudel*, p.491. (Desclée De Brouwer, 1947).
[16] *Art Poétique*, pp.165-6. (Mercure de France, 1913).

blows which nail down Violaine's coffin, they who remain are overwhelmed by joy, that joy which surpasses all joy. Conflict, dramatic elements have vanished ; the action has turned into a lyric flight. In the very presence of death a hymn of praise, exuberant yet restrained, rises, a hymn which takes on a slightly different note with each voice. That of Anne is rich and calm, praising the splendour of the earth ; that of Pierre, more learned but no less mystical, evoking the glory of church building ; that of Jacques, lacking fervour still, heavy with his last human regrets, slow to follow the two souls who wing their flight towards God, but invaded, despite himself, despite his incomprehension, by the mystery of the peace which surrounds him.

And the ringing of the Angelus, symbol of the rebirth of souls and of their acceptance, pealing the news of France's spiritual resurgence over the countryside, strikes the final note :

" Anne : God is made man.

Jacques : He died.

Pierre : He has risen.

(Third stroke of the nuns' bell, then a peal). Pause.

Then is heard, faint, almost indistinguishable, the triple note of the third chime on the heights.

Anne : That isn't the Angelus, it's the bell for Communion.

Pierre : The three notes, like an ineffable sacrifice, are gathered to the breast of the stainless Virgin."

CHAPTER IX.

LYRICISM*

> " For when you speak, like a tree
> which with all its leaves
> Stirs in the silence of mid-day, in us
> little by little peace succeeds to
> thought.
> Through this song without music
> and this word without voice, we
> are attuned to the melody of this
> world."—*La Ville.*

IN this play where tragedy is but little influenced by the
actual events, where the clash between the characters
is less important than the struggles of each individual with
his destiny, a varied harmonious lyricism, rich in imagery
and symbols follows the curve of the action. It is true that,
in the *Tidings*, we no longer find the tempestuous accents,
the verbal exuberance, the strange metaphors of *Tête
d'or.* Here the poetry, more restrained and spiritual, does
not hold up the action ; at the most it occasionally slows it.
There are moreover numerous scenes where the dialogue is
rapid and colloquial, the conversation full of naturalness
and spontaneity or even realism. Such, for instance, is
that where Mara, angry and jealous, forces her mother to
dissuade Violaine from marrying Jacques ; or that where
we hear the lively vivid talk, the rich patois of the simple
folk who await, on the road of Chevoche, the passage of
Jeanne d'Arc and the king. But, as well as these " conversa-

* In this chapter and in the next, for the purposes of illustration, it
has been necessary to quote occasionally lines already cited.

tional " scenes, there are others, and they are numerous, where the voices of the characters are raised in a hymn which is sometimes human, sometimes mystical.

Claudel's lyricism is nearly always closely linked with natural beauty ; he is the poet who sings the splendour of the earth : " The happiness of being a Catholic was in the first place for me to be in communion with the universe."[1] A traveller over the face of the earth he had gazed on the most varied landscapes, yet he remains essentially a native of Tardinois. To him that land, its contours, its colours, its changing lights, its perfumes, the song of its birds, the rustle of its leaves, was destined to be dear beyond all else. Sometimes, in one flash, Claudel seems to capture, to enshrine in a phrase, the vast loveliness of nature. Thus does he show us the varying colours with which the seasons deck the earth : " Green and rose in spring, blue and blond in summer, brown or all white beneath the snow in winter." (p.206).[2]

Most often it is the characters themselves who, completing the stage indications, evoke in brief word-pictures the setting of the play. In the Prologue we glimpse the countryside, indistinct still in the veiled light of dawn ; later, in Act II, we see Violaine, bathed in burning sunlight, coming forth between the flower-laden branches to meet Jacques. And soon, as a contrast to the dazzling setting of this love scene, there comes the nakedness of winter : the land lies white beneath the snow, hoar frost glimmers on the trees beneath the strange, pale, lonely light of the moon. Finally, in Act IV, there is the magnificent evocation of fertile fields ;

[1] *Figaro*, 4th Sept., 1937.
[2] In his vivid use of colour, if in nothing else, Claudel has points of resemblance with A. E. Housman. One remembers the latter's " coloured counties " ; his " cherry hung with snow " ; his lines " Tarnish late on Wenlock Edge, Gold that I shall not see."

the wonder of harvest time and of trees heavy with fruit. This season for Claudel, as for John Keats, is rich, lovely, calm. In the light of the afternoon the land stretches away into the distance and it has borne the promise of its spring. Anne contemplates it :

" The gilded fall
Now
Strips the fruit tree and the vine . . .
And it is near at hand, that evening when he who passes
    beneath the poplars
Will hear the last leaf rustling at the very top." (p.182).

Perpetually, too, the unchanging, changeless background of Monsanvierge with its five towers is recalled to our minds. Sometimes the picture is more vast : we see the whole surrounding district where Pierre de Craon's churches arise, diverse in their beauty but linked to the soil on which they stand, the soil which provided the materials for their construction.

This vision of the world, however, is not merely artistic it remains fundamentally mystical. Whether he contemplates a landscape, a colour, or the effect of light on the countryside, Claudel seeks a hidden meaning. Everything in nature, even the most insignificant object, is important : " Each tree has its personality, each tiny beast its rôle, each voice its place in the symphony."[3] In the variety of the universe the Christian perceives a marvellous unity :

"From the greatest angel who sees us down to the pebble on
        the road, and from one end of our creation to the other
    Everything is continuous."[4]

[3] *Connaissance de l'Est*, p.114. (Mercure de France).
[4] *Cinq grandes Odes*, p.58. (Gallimard).

For this reason man and his background appear to the poet to exist in perfect harmony. In the *Tidings*, all the characters, even Anne during his exile, are firmly rooted in the soil of Tardinois. Pierre is somewhat apart. Although he is far from being insensible to the moving beauty of the earth he lives in another world. Between him and his churches there exist subtle and infinite correspondences. The grandeur of these buildings, his creations, absorbs him so much that we have the impression that it is only with difficulty that he returns to face the ordinary realities of existence. He puts something of his soul into his churches and they, in their turn, form him and spiritualize him. Thus the interior and the exterior world become indissolubly fused. Not only does the earth offer scenes which in themselves are harmonious or magnificent, but all the elements of this concrete world act on the souls of men and therefore play their part in explaining the meaning of the drama.

Lyricism, for Claudel, is not merely vision, it is also movement ; it has the rhythm of life itself. Alongside these passages full of descriptive beauty, often mingled with them, there are others which express thought, emotion, meditation or prayer. "The object of dramatic action is to reveal the interior being in its completeness. Lyricism is the natural expression of a soul which has at last attained to self-knowledge. Lyric rhythm is, in fact, merely the essential vibration of the individual. Thus we see that, as soon as they are *moved*, souls, which appear to be the most obscure, begin to sing, to vibrate."[5]

We could follow the example of many others and attempt those analyses of the internal structure of the rhythm :

[5] Madaule, J., *Le Génie de Paul Claudel*, pp.300-1. (Desclée De Brouwer).

frequency of stress, repetitions of sounds, choice of vowels. Is this not often however a futile and exterior method? " It is in vain," says Paul Valéry, " that we count the steps of the goddess and note their frequency, their average length, we shall not learn from that the secret of her instantaneous grace."[6] Instead of such a detailed study therefore we shall limit ourselves to a few general remarks on the emotional richness of the rhythmic movement and its adaptation to each character.

In order to obtain the liberty, the frankness, the vivacity of the spoken language[7] Claudel created his celebrated " verset " which, through its varying length, has affinities both with prose and poetry. The fluidity of this rhythm permits the expression of the subtlest shades of emotion : a hesitation, a sudden weariness, passions, vehemence, tenderness, peace, prayer ; all bring their own movement, their own life. The " verset " allows the poet to show " psychology through action "[8] or in other words, to sketch character without what he calls " wearisome analysis."[9]

By the use of this medium he avoids all monotony in the lyrical passages ; through his poetry we perceive the personality of each individual with his aspirations, his sufferings, his conflicts.[10] Each voice is heard, different in emotional

[6] Préface. *Anthologie des poètes de la N.R.F.*, p.15. (Gallimard, 1936).
[7] Cf. *Positions et Propositions*, i. pp.60-1. (Gallimard, 2nd ed.). Cf. also *Correspondance de Claudel et Jacques Rivière*, p.127. (Plon-Nourrit, 1926) : " A line of my poetry is never anything except a cry." In this definition he is close to Paul Valéry who says of poetry that it is " the effort to represent or to reconstitute, in articulate language, these things or that thing, which cries, tears, caresses, kisses, sighs endeavour vaguely to express." *Morceaux Choisis*, p.168. (Gallimard, 1930).
[8] *Positions et Propositions*, i, p.65. (Gallimard, 2nd ed.).
[9] *Ibid.*
[10] " Behold, I have created many words and imagined stories, and persons, together in my heart with their different voices." *Magnificat.*

content, in note, in depth and, as we shall see, in symbolism. It is a striking fact that the more a character is actively dramatic the less he is lyrical. There is little poetry in Mara. In gasping, harsh sentences she cries her anger, her revolt, her defiance, her bitter irony or even her lonely and pathetic grief. Violaine, on the other hand, is poetry incarnate. In the Prologue, a happy, innocent child, confident in love to come, she sings her joy :

" Forgive me for being too happy ! because he whom I love

Loves me, and I am sure of him, and I know that he loves me, and all is equal between us !

And because God made me in order that I might be happy and not for evil nor for any sorrow." (p.29).

Later, knowing her separation from Jacques to be inevitable, in a voice still quivering with human regrets, she tells of the beauty and strength of spiritual love :

" I must no longer reserve anything, I must no longer keep for myself

This great, this ineffable secret

.   .   .   .   .   .

So great, Jacques, that in truth

Your heart will be absolutely satisfied,

And you will not ask any more of me,

And we shall never more be torn one from the other.

Such a profound communion,

Jacques, that neither life, nor hell, nor even Heaven will terminate it." (p.95).

Jacques, as we have seen, strikes at the time of his engagement notes of purity, of freshness and of restrained emotion.

After the death of Violaine he utters tortured calls to her who leaves him in solitude. The rhythm here is uneven, expressing sudden exclamations and complaints.

Thus the Claudelian " verset " by its sonority, its movement, its divisions, follows closely the living chain of thought and the fluctuations of the emotions : sometimes quick and abrupt ; sometimes full, slow and grave. In the *Tidings* since the whole play represents a progression towards serenity, the second rhythm is dominant.

Pierre de Craon and Anne Vercors, being more static, more contemplative than the other characters, witnesses to the drama rather than actors therein, lose themselves in long poetic monologues, often forgetful, it would seem, of their listeners. In the beginning Pierre, the passionate Pierre of the Prologue, is still if not an active character at least the echo of one. He proclaims, in tragic tone, his regrets, his sorrows, his aspirations towards peace and death. Already, however, the artist in him is transported in a movement of love by the beauty of his work. Later, pacified and freed from shame, his words become a hymn of thanksgiving when he realizes the superb meaning of his vocation and the splendour of his churches :

" Oh how beautiful is stone and how soft it is in the architect's hands ! and how good and beautiful a thing is his whole completed work !

How faithful is the stone, how it preserves the idea, and what shadows it casts !

And how well a vine looks on the smallest wall, and the rose tree above it when it is in flower,

How beautiful it is, and at the same time how real ! "
(p.199).

Pierre's is the exultation of the penitent who has found his appropriate place and who has discovered a wonderful fullness in life. He symbolizes those artists of the Middle Ages who united, in an often anonymous community, to raise to the skies the testimony of their faith.

Anne, the most lyrical of all the characters, praises turn by turn the richness of the past, the beauty of family life, the glory of the earth, the union between God and the toiler, the joy of the exile who returns. At the end of the play, the old man's hymn, although in parts it is somewhat long-drawn out and although the metaphors are occasionally disconcerting, rises in a mystical effusion which gives to us an echo of the moving depth and beauty of the Bible and of the Liturgy. The magnificence of the world, the nothingness of man before God, the infinite goodness of God to man—such are his themes :

" Violaine ! Elisabeth ! Soon I shall be with you again !
    As for you, Jacques, in your turn do your task as I
        have done mine ! The end is close ;
    Behold, the end of all is given me, of the day, of the
        year and of life !
    It is six o'clock. The shadow of the Grès-qui-va-boire
        reaches the stream.
    Winter comes, night comes. A little bit of night now,
    A short watch still ! " (pp.201-2).
" The sun and I, side by side,
    Have toiled, and the result of our toil does not concern
        us.
    Mine is finished . . .
    And herein, for him who knows it, lies peace and joy
    And sorrow in equal parts." (p.203).

It is the triumphant hymn of faith of the man who has measured all the value of sacrifice and the meaning and richness of Christian life. It breathes the peace of one who casts a last tender glance towards those whom he loves, towards the beauty of the world ; he is already however journeying towards that Paradise of which he has caught a glimpse in the night of his old age and solitude. His slow, grave voice has the rhythm of an incantation, the majesty of Plain Chant, and it expresses the deepest, the most mystical thoughts of the whole play. In Anne's words there is mingled lucid human wisdom and the profound emotion of the Christian who is very close to God, who is sure of God with a certainty which vibrates with love, gratitude and joy.

The play is a symphony of diverse voices, harmonising, superimposed : sometimes pathetic, more often exultant with a grave and mystical happiness. In this work where " in the heart of the most peaceful dialogue drama perpetually rumbles ",[11] Claudel has achieved a perfect fusion of lyricism and of action. The poetry of the background, the splendour, the radiant light of the pictures, make the poignant intensity of the spiritual atmosphere more tragic. The hymns which surge forth from these souls reveal the depths of interior life which each one bears within himself. Thrown into relief by lyricism we perceive a psychological complexity which is strikingly and movingly true. The conflicts between ideas and feelings, between nature and grace are shown in a new light by these lyrical passages. Above all they reveal the effort of the soul straining, sometimes unconsciously, towards God.

---

[11] Blanchet, A., Foreword to *Pages de Prose*, p.13. (Gallimard, 1944).

CHAPTER X

SYMBOLISM AND IMAGERY

> " Imagery is not a portion of the
> whole, it is the symbol of it, it is
> like a key."—*Art Poétique*.

IF, as we have already seen, the rhythm, the movement
and the tonality of the different voices reveal the interior
life of the characters, an extraordinary richness of metaphors
and of symbols allows us to penetrate still further into the
secret of these souls, to distinguish with greater clarity the
mystical meaning of the play. Through an intimate and
mysterious union rhythm and imagery complete each
other and form a perfect whole, heavy with poetic beauty
and with the essence of humanity. The poet has not far to
seek. He need only glance about him : " Water, air, the sun,
the sky, animals, plants, a lamp, a child's face, a wall,
a door. Heavens ! how beautiful it is and what echoes it
awakens in us."[1] Continually the exterior world provides
similitudes with the interior world and becomes thus an
explanation of the things of the soul.

In this play—itself a symbol in action—a gesture, an
object, a garment, a scene can conceal a profound meaning.
Thus in the Prologue Violaine herself opens the great
door of the barn " with difficulty " so that a landscape, still
night-enveloped but breathing already of the dawn, is
revealed. She thus shows to Pierre the passage from shadows

[1] Letter to Louis Gillet, quoted in *Claudel Présent*, p.72. (Egloff, 1943).

to light, from sin to grace and to hope. Jacques' ring, which Violaine gives to Pierre to help the building of St. Justice, is a symbol of her yet unconscious renunciation of happiness in earthly love : " Take it quickly for I shall not have the strength to part with it." (p.13).

The dalmatic which Violaine wears for her betrothal sets her already apart and gives a foreglimpse of her life of solitude and sacrifice : " It is not the attire of a woman but the garment of him who offers up sacrifice at the altar." (p.93).

For Pierre leprosy is the symbol of his sin ; for Violaine it becomes a source of penance and the sign of her ardent charity. When Aubaine is miraculously restored to life her eyes which, says Mara, " alone are mine ", have now become the blue eyes of Violaine. Thus has Violaine in some sort communicated her own spiritual life to the child. Violaine later admits to Jacques that at the moment of the miracle she experienced the pangs of child birth. In this way does Claudel show the fruitfulness of sacrifice which, though apparently turned away from life, is nevertheless the spiritual channel through which life continues.

Significant too is the setting of Violaine's death. It is autumn, the gilded season of fecundity, of harvest, of fruit ; the moment when all those who remain behind are spiritually enriched by the sacrifice of the leper girl.

But alongside this symbolism which arises from the setting or the action we find what might be called spoken symbols, waves of imagery which correspond to the unfolding of the thoughts, the feelings of the characters. Continually Claudel establishes correspondences, analogies betwixt the spiritual and the exterior world. In a flow of metaphors everything becomes concrete. The depth of a feeling, the intensity of an emotion are made visual and transposed into the world of line, of colour, of sound or of perfume.

For instance Pierre de Craon's bitter moral solitude is translated by the moving contrast which exists between the majesty of his cathedrals and the humble construction in which he had dreamed of enclosing all his human happiness :

" So many proud roof-ridges ! Shall I never see that of
    my little house amidst the trees?
  So many spires whose moving shadows write the hour
    across a whole town. Shall I never design an oven and
    a children's room? " (p.32).

For Anne the joy of return after a long exile is expressed in its essence by the sweetness of a familiar scent :

" And all the spices of exile are as little to me
  Compared to this walnut leaf which I crush between
    my fingers." (p.179).

The abundance, the richness, the variety of these images force us to make a choice ; a complete study of Claudel's use of symbolism in this play would require a volume ; we shall therefore merely point out some striking instances.

In this profusion of images some are strange, obscure, far-fetched ; that is however an exception. Usually they are transparently simple. They spring from the experience of the characters who voice them, from humble daily reality, from the land.

After Violaine's death Jacques, still rebellious, contemplates the life of solitude which awaits him :

" . . . I shall have to
  Live and continue ! Like an animal that is seized by the
    horn and whose head is dragged from the manger,

Like a horse that, in the evening, is unharnessed and
driven off with a blow on the croup." (p.183).

With humility Anne measures the space which separates
him from the daughter who has just died, her death illumi-
nated by the gentle rays of holiness. From her he feels that
he is as far removed " as the smoky fire of this farm is from
the morning star " (p.196). In an equally homely picture
he evokes the paternal but severe judgment of God :

" Here is the evening ! Have pity on every man, Lord,
    at this moment when, having finished his task, he
    stands before You like a child whose hands are being
    examined.
Mine are clean ! " (p.207).

Other comparisons are harsh, almost crude :

" Oh, when you speak of your Violaine, it's all sugar,
    It's like a cherry that one sucks, the moment before
    spitting out the stone !
But Mara the magpie ! she is hard as iron, as bitter as
    the wild cherry ! " (p.54).

All the hate-filled anger, the jealous rancour of Mara, all
her cruel self-knowledge, are contained in the opposition
of these short, biting sentences. Later when her spirit,
despite momentary violence, is broken, she sees all the
earthly heaviness of her being ; pathetically lucid she knows
herself to be without grace, without beauty :

". . . ah, it is not the flower in season,
    But that which is beneath the flowers which fade, the
    earth itself, the miserly earth beneath the grass, the
    earth of which there is never any lack ! " (pp.190-1).

Alongside these comparisons full of sap, heavy with the scent which rises from the soil of Tardinois, there are others which are discreet, spiritual, disincarnate. Just as Prouhèze in the *Satin Slipper* is continually likened to a star, symbolic of distant alluring beauty, so too in the *Tidings* do we find a similar *motif*. Violaine's name evokes for us a flower ; only after a detailed study do we realize why. The other characters continually liken her to blossoms. Her father calls her " this gentle narcissus " ; Jacques hails her as a " beautiful lily ", a flower of light ; she is the " supreme flower ", " the flower in its season ", finally she is " a solemn lily ". Her leprosy itself is tranfigured and becomes " this flower of silver ". Violaine in the scene with Jacques which opens with the lovely passage : " O hail, my betrothed, through the flowery branches ", makes the comparison :

". . . What do you ask of me more?

What does one ask of a flower

Except that, for an instant, it be beautiful and perfumed, and afterwards it will be ended.

The flower is short lived, but the joy which for an instant it gave

Is not of those things which have either beginning or end ! " (p.92)[2]

And the symbol is reinforced by Anne Vercors' words to Jacques when the latter seeks flowers to strew on the dead girl :

" There are no flowers, now there is only fruit." (p.185)

[2] " It is not the rose ! It is its perfume
Breathed for an instant which is eternal." *Cantate à trois Voix*, p.23. (Gallimard, 1943).

As the blossoms on the trees have been transformed so too has Violaine attained to her supreme development.

These repetitions owe nothing to chance; whether Claudel be conscious of it or not, they correspond to a spiritual reality. They follow each other, sometimes slightly different, one comparison adding to the other, casting new light on it, uniting their meaning to form a sort of synthesis, striking in its simplicity. Eternally Violaine will be an exquisite flower of beauty and of purity just as Prouhèze will be a distant, inaccessible star, shining in the immensity of the night.

There is nothing forced in this succession of symbols. Sometimes one image gives birth to another. From the theme of the flower comes that of perfume. While the " lily ", the " gentle narcissus ", evoke grace, feminine fragility, youth and purity, perfume corresponds to a more secret reality. It represents the soul, spiritual life, that which is undying. However intangible, however subtle is this sign it is nevertheless perceptible. For Pierre it is the symbol of Violaine's spiritual richness :

" Thus the scent of the hidden soul, like that of a mint leaf, is what reveals its virtue." (p.18).

But in even the purest beings passions remain ; the flesh may stifle the spirit. Only when Violaine's body is destroyed, eaten away by leprosy, does the soul triumph over all that is earthly :

" Jacques ! understand me.
   Of what use is the best perfume in a closed vase? It is of no use . . .
   Now I am utterly broken, and the perfume breathes forth." (p.65-6).

95

When Pierre bears in his arms Violaine, dying, now a victim, offered to God as a sacrifice, the immaterial and ineffable beauty of the spiritual being, liberated from the flesh, is manifest in all its reality :

" And the scent of Paradise, between my arms, breathed forth from this broken tabernacle." (p.197).

In the world of Claudelian symbols, birds assume a special significance. They represent that which is spiritual ; chosen beings athirst for purity, all those who have lost something of heavy human materialism, all those who direct their flight towards God, who " go directly to heaven ". Monsanvierge is referred to as " a dovecot " ; its inhabitants are " those murmuring birds ". Jacques, on the other hand, is " a wingless man ". Violaine is compared to a lark. In the joy of her radiant youth, in her free flight towards God, she is as that speck of moving light lost in the light of heaven : " with wings spread wide, the little vehement cross, like the seraphim who are wings only, footless, a shrill voice before the throne of God." (p.28).

The mystery of death, liberation from narrow earthly limitations, is twice represented in the *Tidings* by a door which suddenly gives way. When Jacques, in despair at Violaine's coming death, is being comforted, she describes to him his own death, the prelude to their eternal spiritual union :

" And then, when it will be your turn and when you see the great door creak and stir, it is I on the other side who come after." (p.175).

Thus, as for Pierre de Craon, it will be the end of a long and weary exile, a moment which he will ardently await. For

Pierre, however, it is even more significant : a vision, even if still shadowy and imprecise, of the glory of heaven, a desire for annihilation in the Divine Love :

" Soon the time will come when another door will melt away.

When he who has pleased but few here below falls asleep, his work finished, sheltered by the eternal and divine wings.

When already through translucent walls appears on all sides dark Paradise.

And when the censers of the night mingle their perfume with the odour of the filthy wick which is being extinguished." (p.19).

In this series of complex and fluid comparisons the visual becomes olfactory. The last moment when the soul takes flight from the body is symbolised by the strange opposition of two scents : one, violently realistic, describes with contempt corrupt and wretched flesh ; the other, with delicate beauty, calls up already the ineffable sweetness of eternal joy.

Such comparisons are more than mere illustrations, more than the concrete presentation of an idea. In their astonishing complexity they sometimes surpass thought, they reveal unexpected but real links and they possess a psychological and emotional content and a poetic beauty impossible in purely abstract expression. They

" rise, expand, envelop us, communicate to us their vibrations . . . We only have to accumulate them to understand, for they penetrate us from all sides at the same time, uttering in many simultaneous ways the same truth."[3]

[3] Rivière, Jacques. *Etudes*, p.69. (N.R.F., 1936).

Even if there are a few examples of obscurity, Claudel's symbolism remains on the whole absolutely intelligible. However complex a comparison may appear it is illumined by an internal light. It is by a slow gradual appreciation that we must penetrate into this world of " signs " for intuition, not logic, dominates.

> " The magic formulae of the poet cannot be employed in cold blood ; all the imagination, all the sensitiveness of the reader must come into play and run high in order to penetrate the vast mass of allusions, of analogies, of correspondences by means of which the poet evokes the phantom of poetry and one must find in oneself phenomena analogous to those of which the poet speaks."[4]

By that means we can arrive at a greater understanding of ourselves and at a luminous insight into the profound meaning of life : " You explain nothing, O Poet, but through you all things become explicable to us."[5]

[4] Carrouges, Michel, *Eluard et Claudel*, p.31. (Ed. du Seuil, 1945).
[5] *La Ville*, p.204. (Mercure de France, 1929).

CHAPTER XI.

POETIC THEORY AND AFFILIATION

> " But you, Coeuvre, who are you and
> of what use are you? "—*La Ville*.

IN most French writers there is a didactic tendency
which causes poets to present side by side with their
creative work a statement of their theory, their doctrine.
In each generation, treatises or manifestoes have defined or
proclaimed new ideas. Whether the intention was to attack
a rival code of aesthetics or merely to arrive at a better
understanding of the secrets of poetic inspiration, these
theoricians have been actuated by a desire for perfection.
This dream of literary renewal, this longing to breathe a new
spirit into ancient forms moved Du Bellay to write his
Deffence et Illustration de la langue française, Hugo to publish
his Preface to *Cromwell* or Paul Valéry to analyse artistic
problems with brilliant subtlety.

Claudel in his turn, with wonderful penetration, gives
us aesthetic meditations. He never wearies of explaining to
us both his conception of poetry and the mysterious
spiritual activity which precedes the creation of his work
Not only is his doctrine analysed in the *Art Poétique* and the
Cinq grandes Odes, we find it everywhere. Sometimes we are
given an abstract, closely thought-out exposition ; sometimes a lyrical outburst or again a concrete, living presentation (for instance the parable of Animus and Anima[1]) or else

---

[1] *Positions et Propositions*, i, pp.55-57. (Gallimard, 2nd ed.).

a dialogue, a few words on the lips of one of his characters by way of simple and direct confidence. Claudel has never ceased to study all the varied domains of the literature and art of many countries for his mind is avid of knowledge and interested in the most diverse problems. This poet, daring and sometimes obscure in his lyrical flights, is one of the best-read men of his period. All his life he has pushed farther and farther his Biblical studies. He is steeped in classical culture. With infinite penetration he has written on Chinese art and theatre, Japanese poetry, Dante, Dutch painting. Certain aspects of English literature appeal to him, especially Milton, Blake, Keats and Coventry Patmore.

In him there is a critic whose likes and dislikes are very pronounced. His ideas are often in their first expression paradoxical but he may later on review them and give to them more subtlety and precision. Always however he approaches the work which he is studying in a direct spontaneous, we might almost say " Bergsonian " manner, and from this contact he draws fresh, independent interpretations. He analyses his own conception of poetry in words which are sometimes too heavy with meaning, too condensed, but which, on the other hand, sometimes attain to perfect lucidity. He shows there not only the union between author and reader, between thought and expression[2]; not only the technical aspects of the craft of poetry, prosody, versification, rhythm ; he has also, as an intellectual, a psychologist, a Christian, defined the importance of selected themes, the function of the writer, the mystery of poetic creation.

[2] " The words which I use
They are everyday words and
They are not the same." *Cinq grandes Odes*, p.120. (Gallimard).

In a study as limited in scope as this it has seemed best to confine ourselves to some aspects of the last problems.

.   .   .   .   .   .

Anything, provided it be regarded in a certain way, is matter for poetry. " Open your eyes ! the world is still intact ; it is virgin as at the first day, as fresh as milk."[3] The universe offers its inexhaustible riches to man. It is useless to seek the extraordinary, the exceptional : humble reality suffices. The world is there with its simple and moving beauty. "A true poet has not the slightest need of bigger stars or more beautiful roses."[4] A secret understanding of things is alone necessary. Pensée, the blind girl of *Le Père humilié*, possesses this attitude of silence and meditation, that is why she can say : " everything touches me in my innermost soul."[5] To Claudel, the splendour of the world is a source of endless joy.

" I shall never believe," he wrote in 1920, " that nature in her invariable and majestic order gives us lessons of anguish and of despair ; quite naturally the believer finds himself in complete harmony with her."[6]

That is why Claudel misses nothing : this realist discerns the simplest, the most fugitive forms of beauty. All the loveliness of the world takes on a deep meaning since we discover there the presence of God. Yet there is no pantheism in this vision of nature. For him, each object is simply incapable of an existence independent of its Creator.

In Claudel's eyes, the mission of the poet is at once proud

[3] *Art Poétique*, p.25. (Mercure de France, 1913).
[4] *Positions et Propositions*, i, p.169. (Gallimard, 2nd ed.).
[5] *Le Père humilié*, p.16. (Gallimard, 6th ed.).
[6] *Positions et Propositions*, ii, p.138. (Gallimard).

and humble, since, before all else, he must be a " witness " before God and yet he must rediscover the initial unity and harmony of the universe. He asks of God the strength to efface himself so that he may simply serve :

" Let me only find the proper word,
Let me only breathe forth
This word from my heart and, having said it, die."[7]

Repeatedly, he expresses this desire to abstract himself from his work, to be " among men as a faceless man."[8] A difficult attitude to maintain since it is necessary to achieve the most perfect result possible. The same self-detachment is revealed in a confidence made to André Gide in 1905 :

" I attach absolutely no value to the literary quality of my work. Frizeau[9] was the first one who, brought back to God by my dramas because he saw religion dominating everything in them, made me think that I haven't written in vain. The literary beauty of my work has no other significance for me than that found by a workman who is aware of having performed his task well ; I simply did my best ; but, had I been a carpenter, I should have been just as conscientious in planing a plank properly as I have been in writing properly."[10]

Sometimes, moreover, he feels crushed by the splendour which he wishes to express. He measures his limitations and his unworthiness :

" Make me, who with my voice create eternal things, oh make me to be wholly

[7] *Cinq grandes Odes*, p.85. (Gallimard).
[8] *Cinq grandes Odes*, p.163. (Gallimard).
[9] A French book-collector and art-lover who was one of the first admirers of Claudel.
[10] Gide, André, *The Journals*, p.163. (New York, 1947).

This voice, a word completely intelligible !
Free me from the enslaving weight of this inert matter !
So make me more clear ! Free me from these hateful
    shadows ! And grant that at last I may be
All that which within me is obscurely desired ! "[11]

This curious poetic doctrine most often develops into an ardent prayer, a dialogue with God. For Claudel, the vocation of poet can be misused or betrayed ; for this reason he never loses sight of the difficulties of his task. Isolation might perhaps present a simpler solution but the poet's function is not to turn his back on the world, on the contrary, it is to live there :

" Lord, You did not put me aside like a hot-house plant,
    Like the black monk beneath his cowl and hood who
        each morning blossoms all in gold for Mass at
        sunrise,
But You planted me in the heaviest of soil."[12]

It is through things that he must discover God and yet he must be in some sort detached from things in order that nothing in him be refractory to spiritual light.

Just as he does not separate himself from the material universe so he avoids isolation from men, his brothers :

" If the astronomer, with heart a-throb, night-long with
    his telescope
    Peers at Mars' face as intently as a coquette at her
        mirror,
    How much more important than the greatest star must
        be to me
    Your lowliest child made to Your own image?

[11] *Cinq grandes Odes*, pp.62-3. (Gallimard).
[12] *Ibid*, p.93.

Mercy is not the vain gift of that which we have already,
    it is a passion like science,
It is, like science, a discovery—the discovery of Your
    Face in the hearts You made.
If all Your stars are necessary to me, how much more
    all my brothers? "[13]

The creature who, in appearance, is the most wretched, the
most surely lost, is still a member of Christ's Mystical Body.
Each individual is, in a sense, responsible for all. Between
men there must exist a link which is nothing other than the
Communion of Saints.

" Not one of our brothers, even if he desire it, is capable of
    completely withdrawing himself from us ; and in the
    coldest miser, in the prostitute, in the most filthy
    drunkard, there is an immortal soul, divinely engaged
    in breathing and which, excluded from the light of day,
    practises nocturnal adoration. I hear them speaking
    when we speak, weeping when I kneel down. I accept
    all : I take them all, I understand them all, there is not
    a single one of them that I don't need or that I can do
    without ! "[14]

The mission of the poet is therefore to study with loving
attention man and his sufferings. His rôle is far from being
passive. To look on at life, even as an understanding
spectator, would be merely another form of isolation and
egoism. The Christian poet desires to assist in the healing of
an unhappy world.

" Yes, we must come to the aid of this creation which
    moans and which needs us. In the first place we must

[13] *Ibid*, p.162.
[14] *Conversations dans le Loir-et-Cher*, Dimanche. (Gallimard).

come to the aid of humanity but we must also come to the aid of the forest, we must come to the aid of the bramble which asks to become a rose . . . Placed between God and the earth, we must come to the aid of both ".[15]

His task is therefore spiritual, an effort necessary in order that the beauty of the world be disclosed, that man may be touched and that God be revealed to him.

Continuing his meditation, Claudel contemplates in himself the birth and growth of his work. Usually the poet is seized and borne off by the sudden invasion of an irresistible force. At the moment of inspiration, he is compared to a young girl, all a-quiver, waiting to be carried off on horseback on a mad ride through the wind and the night. She experiences no regret for the peaceful home which she is leaving for " all her heart is uplifted by love of life and by the great cosmic force."[16] But inspiration is also the fresh, spontaneous flight of the soul (Anima) which, having disengaged itself from servile toil, " advances amidst pure things with an infinitely light and rapid step."[17] It is at the moment when it becomes " docile to the divine hand which leads it ",[18] when it has attained to meditation and silence that it sings " all alone, behind the closed door . . . a strange and wonderful song."[19] The mind (Animus) whose rôle is far from being without importance, is exasperated because it does not always understand the meaning of this secret melody.

[15] *Ibid.*
[16] *Cinq grandes Odes*, p.117. (Gallimard).
[17] *Positions et Propositions*, i, p.99. (Gallimard, 2nd ed.).
[18] *Ibid.*
[19] *Ibid*, p.57.

Whether it be tempestuous or more gently intimate, poetic or artistic creation corresponds to an imperious necessity :

" Do you believe for a moment ", wrote Claudel in 1912 to Jacques Rivière, " that Shakespeare or Dostoievsky, or Rubens, or Titian, or Wagner did their work *for art's sake*? No ! They did it to free themselves of a great incubus of living matter, *opus non factum*. And certainly not to colour a cold, artificial design by borrowings from reality."[20]

True poetry is then something new and spontaneous ; it is the opposite of the dry ingeniousness of the *virtuoso*. It is " that language which comes from the soul and returns to the heart."[21] Inspiration alone however cannot make a great poet. In his fine speech on Dante, Claudel in 1921 expressed his thought clearly : to this powerful force which raises the soul must be added " not only perfect good will, simplicity and good faith, but also exceptional natural gifts, controlled and guided by an intelligence at once bold, prudent and subtle."[22]

Thus in Claudel's work can be discovered a philosophy of which we have tried to sum up the essential points. If his ideas do not always correspond to our own conception of poetry that is of no account: " a poet does not pursue truth, he pursues *his* truth and this pursuit is pathetic."[23] The important point is however that Claudel has devoted much reflection to these literary problems which for him are fraught with significance.

[20] *Correspondance avec Jacques Rivière*, p.248. (Plon-Nourrit, 1926).
[21] *Pages de Prose* (edited by A. Blanchet), p.107. (Gallimard, 1944).
[22] *Positions et Propositions*, i, pp.162-3. (Gallimard, 2nd ed.).
[23] Duhamel G. *Paul Claudel*, p.15. (Mercure de France).

At the same time that he constructed his poetic doctrine he continued his creative work, thus testing his theories. If sometimes he tries to defend himself against certain accusations[24] more generally it is in order to satisfy himself rather than to enlighten the public that he meditates on these different problems. Ceaselessly, under varying forms, he asks himself the same questions, and always he discovers the same answers. In this way, despite some contradictions in matters of detail, his attitude does not change, it merely becomes more definite, and his judgments form a coherent whole of an incontestable originality. It does more than cast light on the work, it reveals the man. By its absolute sincerity, its penetration and its depth it also reveals the Christian, the " witness of God ", the strength and radiance of a living faith.

.   .   .   .   .   .

Another question which is raised is whether the Claudelian aesthetic creed allows us to discern the position of the poet in French literary tradition? to what school can this independent genius be connected? " With him we must get used to a certain abruptness ", says Louis Gillet, " he must be approached as if he were a mountain, a sort of island in the middle of the sea."[25] This solitude is not however the sign of disdainful pride. No one is more prone than Claudel to entertain great and fervent admiration of others. It is true nevertheless that he presents the aspect of a lonely revolutionary. Moved by the impulsion of his genius he

[24] Cf. for instance the first part of the *Maison fermée* (*Cinq grandes Odes*) where he justifies his often criticized obscurity and where he touches on the problem of a poet's union with his readers.
[25] Gillet, Louis, *Claudel-Péguy*, p.17. (Sagittaire, 1946).

seeks new lands, not in order to achieve notoriety but because he remains dissatisfied, since every instinct in him craves something fresh. This attitude is the result of a sincere quest and is a sign of strength and optimism. This struggle against tradition appears somewhat repellent to contemporaries ; but is not literary history composed of a series of revolts? The passage of time often attenuates for us the violent opposition between one literary period and its immediate predecessors. The Renaissance despised the simplicity of the Middle Ages ; Classicism proclaimed its scorn of Rabelais and Ronsard ; Romanticism, in its turn, disdained Classicism and especially the pseudo-classicism of the 18th century. And the succession of ruptures continued with the Parnassians and the Symbolists. Such conflicts are a sign of literary rebirth, heralds of reform.

Claudel in turn takes his place amidst the great rebels. His complaints are sometimes severe and exaggerated ; but his common sense, his sure judgment often cause him to correct some of his affirmations later.

In the first place he rejects the doctrines of the 17th century, the narrowness of its rules, so much does he fear for himself a too-severe discipline. What is more astonishing is that he rebels against the very inspiration of the great century of French literature, judging it to be at the same time too pagan and too spiritualized.[26] This criticism in no way interferes with his admiration of certain classical writers or even with his recognition of the value of the harmonious play of all the faculties, of " perfect composition " and of " the spirit of moderation ". In 1910 he answered

[26] Cf. Tonquédec, J. de., *L'Oeuvre de Paul Claudel*, p.162. (Beauchesne, 3rd ed.).

a query put by *Paris-Journal* : " In the production of a work of art judgment, intelligence, the sense of order and proportion, scrupulous attachment to the proposed goal play a part as important as that of the imagination proper."[27] In truth, Claudel is too profoundly French to have escaped the influence of the Classical age. It is in vain that even the most rebellious, the most tumultuous French writers of genius attempt to escape : a sure instinct tells them, despite themselves, of the value of great richness of imagination and of feeling disciplined and ordered.[28] Despite their revolts they know full well that this discretion, this moderation does not represent impoverishment.

> " Because the form is restrictive ", wrote Baudelaire with his splendid mental acuteness, " the idea issues with a greater intensity . . . Have you noticed that a patch of sky seen through a vent hole, or between two chimneys or two rocks, or under an archway gives a deeper perception of the infinite than a wide panorama seen from a mountain top?"[29]

And Charles Péguy, despite the fact that he deserves the reproach of being disorderly and exaggerated in his writings, asks himself: " How can one avoid being classical? "[30] Claudel himself understood the necessity of pruning, of choosing, of eliminating. After the first sudden invasion of

[27] Quoted in *Revue critique des idées et des livres*, 25th Aug., 1910.
[28] André Gide expressed this idea with penetration : " The classical work is beautiful and strong only in so far as it represents disciplined romanticism." *Incidences*, p.38. Or again : " The work gains in beauty according as the conquered thing was more rebellious." *Incidences*, p.217. (Gallimard, 1924).
[29] *Lettres*, 1841-1866, p.238. (Mercure de France, 1917).
[30] *Note conjointe sur M. Descartes précédée de la note sur M. Bergson*, p.69. (Gallimard, 1923).

inspiration, after the poet's initial yielding to the great force which bears him away, he measures all the richness which discipline brings. Though he appreciates the fecundity of the powerful inspiration which floods his being, he adds this unexpected prayer :

" But you, do not abandon me,
  O moderating Muses."[31]

If his accusations against the seventeenth century are often sweeping and excessive, his respect for intelligence and reason, his detestation of exaggeration, his solid common-sense, his admiration for certain writers of the classical age, betray despite appearances numerous links with the literature and the outlook of *le grand siècle*.

On the whole, Claudel is less severe for the doctrine of Romanticism which cast aside the rules of unity and allowed in the theatre the mingling of tragic and comic. On the other hand however, he remarks on the mediocrity of the majority of its writers : " The misfortune is that French romantic poetry was written by insufficiently endowed people."[32] He knows that literary periods of enthusiasm and lyricism are not, of necessity, the most fundamentally rich ; much insignificance can be cloaked beneath high-sounding words. The artificiality, the declamatory style, the verbosity of so much Romantic poetry often represent merely " a lessening of quality and density."[33] True originality does not consist in the desire for the exotic, the exceptional ; neither does it manifest itself by unbridled imagination and emotion. Claudel is too catholic, in the

[31] *Cinq grandes Odes*, p.18. (Gallimard).
[32] *Nouvelles littéraires*, 18 April, 1925.
[33] *Positions et propositions*, i, p.34. (Gallimard, 2nd ed.).

wide sense of the word, to be able to admire narcissism, or to welcome egotistical confessions where the individual is absorbed in the contemplation of self.

Finally, his greatest reproach to Romanticism is the emptiness, the limitations of its inspiration : its poetry is bereft of God, of hope and of joy. Victor Hugo's most usual feeling " is terror, a sort of panic-filled contemplation."[34] Through this whole waste land of Romanticism, as later in almost all the literature of the nineteenth century, " we find only despair, pessimism, nightmare, bitterness, frenzy, fury, the mind possessed by the most hideous spectacles in order to culminate—to-day—in the stammerings of imbecility."[35]

It is very evident that Claudel's lyricism, vibrant with life as it is, has no point of contact with the cold, hard, impeccable poetry of the Parnassian group. One is however forced to ask one's self to what extent he belongs to the Symbolist school, with its obscure dreams and its haunted quest for pure music. Baudelaire's poetry filled his youth with ecstasy and for long years he was moved by the pathetic sight of this " soul swollen with desires, with memories and with remorse."[36] He loves the nostalgic melody of Verlaine ; the poignant voice of " somebody who remembers and who, eyes closed, sings."[37] He admits having admired Mallarmé ; but if he recognizes a master it is Rimbaud, " that wild madman, that vagabond, that indomitable creature, that outlaw."[38] Rimbaud remains the

[34] *Ibid*, p.45.
[35] *Ibid*, p.53.
[36] *Ibid*, p.37.
[37] *Ibid*, p.171
[38] *Un poète regarde la Croix*, p.269. (Gallimard, 24th ed.).

one man about whom, until his life's end, he will think with " an infinite gratitude, a profound affection."[39] For " it is he, " Claudel affirms, " who saved me from Hell and the University."[40]

And yet, despite this twofold acknowledgement of a spiritual and artistic debt, despite his cult for this child of genius, Claudel remains apart. If he has preserved the musical phrase, the love of the mysterious so characteristic of the Symbolists, he is separated from them by the healthy and robust attitude so noticeable in his writings, by his instinctive horror of that which is exaggerated and troubled, by his rejection of the too etherial beauty where the Symbolists often lost themselves. This countryman is a realist, for his roots are deep sunk in the land :

" And I, I produce by ploughing, the seasons toil hard
    at my heavy, difficult soil.
Fundamental, compact,
I have given myself over to the harvests, I am sub-
    missive to agriculture."[41]

Claudel's passionate love of colour, of light, of scents, has in it something physical, even carnal. Nevertheless, behind the beautiful, outward shell, is that which essentially he desires to seize : the intimate soul which animates all things. Troubled dreams, morbid searchings in the dregs of conscience have no place in his work. In his plays the

[39] *Ibid.*

[40] *Ibid.* Claudel is not the only Frenchman to protest against a system of higher education which was characterised for too long by the mark of Taine's and Renan's influence, by political pre-occupations, by the unscrupulous ambition of certain individuals. As well as Claudel one thinks immediately of Henri Massis, Alfred de Tarde, and of the long, epic struggle of Charles Péguy against the " intellectual party ".

[41] *Cinq grandes Odes*, p.31. (Gallimard).

characters are living beings of flesh and blood, possessed of intense vitality. This idealist whose eyes are turned towards the supernatural never relinquishes his grasp on reality. Especially he does not desire an empty symbolism which believes that it can do without God. He knows that the world " speaks to us humbly, joyously of its own absence, but also of the eternal presence of somebody else, that is, its Creator."[42]

The effort to connect a poet at all costs to a certain school is often a vain task :

> " To descriminate schools, of art, of literature, is, of course, part of the obvious business of literary criticism : but, in the world of literary production, it is easy to be overmuch occupied concerning them. For, in truth, the legitimate contention is, not of one age or school of literary art against another, but of all successive schools alike, against the stupidity which is dead to the substance, and the vulgarity which is dead to form."[43]

Indeed, Claudel belongs to no school. If he owes much to Rimbaud, we can say that his debt to Homer, to Virgil, to Dante is scarcely smaller. Whatever his admiration, his strong personality makes him impervious to any vital influence. Moreover, his travels, his long residence in various foreign countries, by making his visits to Paris merely intermittant, kept him free from the influence of French literary circles. His work grew in solitude and thus he was saved from artistic infatuation to which he might have succumbed. In this he was a little like Francis Jammes who

[42] *Positions et Propositions*, i. p.206. (Gallimard, 2nd ed.).
[43] Pater, Walter, *Appreciations*, p.274. (Macmillan, 1931).

disliked Paris and who, in his distant province in the Pyrenees, was as far from the coteries as was Claudel in China.

Yet despite this solitude in which he creates his powerful and original work, it is certainly true that he experienced certain influences : " The individual, in art any more than in society, does not live alone."[44] What one can say is that these influences never reach the essential depths, never encumber this independent man. On the other hand they are so varied in their nature that inevitably they are dispersed, inefficacious. Essentially Claudel remains himself. He possessed a power, a strength which enabled him to create a new poetic form, deeply human, deeply moving, having its origin in his very soul ; an eternal, original and living work which expresses Claudel's whole being. The object of poetry " is not, as is often stated, dreams, illusions or ideas. It is this holy reality, given once and for all, in the midst of which we are placed. It is the universe of visible things to which Faith adds that of the invisible things."[45]

[44] Tonquédec, Joseph de, *L'Oeuvre de Paul Claudel*, p.185. (Beauchesne, 3rd ed.).
[45] *Positions et Propositions*, i, p.165. (Gallimard, 2nd ed.).

CHAPTER XII.

THE MESSAGE OF PAUL CLAUDEL

> " At Claudel's call the world began
> to awaken."—*Claudel*, V. Bindel.

" YOU have brought us happiness—that somewhat too lonely happiness, the enemy of any literature which denies it, that happiness which isolates you in the midst of a generation."[1] These words of François Mauriac are especially true to-day. After the tragedy of two wars and in a world dominated by a defeatist passivity, by an aspiration towards nothingness, by a desolate scepticism, by so many tragic and despairing philosophies which proclaim the absurdity of life,[2] Claudel's characteristics stand out more clearly than ever : his feeling for nobility and heroism, the invincible certainty of his faith, the exultation of the Christian who marches towards eternity. In 1930 Claudel himself, in a letter to Jacques Madaule, defined his attitude :

> " You have seen clearly the general idea of my life and of my vocation : a great desire for and a great uprising towards divine joy and an attempt to link the whole world to it . . . to recall the entire Universe to its ancient rôle of Paradise."[3]

[1] Speech of François Mauriac at the reception of Claudel at the French Academy, 13th March, 1947.
[2] As well as Existentialism, the " Philosophy of Nausea " as J. P, Sartre calls it, there is also the pessimism of P. Valéry, of André Gide, of André Malraux, of Julien Green, the spiritual anguish of Marcel Proust or of Jean Anouilh.
[3] Letter-Preface to *Le Génie de Paul Claudel*, p.10 (Desclée De Brouwer).

And yet this man had known a bitter pessimism in his youth. After a happy childhood the ardent, lonely boy had found himself face to face with the sorrow of the world, the horror of death. For a long time he struggled desperately within the shadows of the " materialistic gaol ". It was " those sad eighties "[4] of the dying nineteenth century which raised to the skies such idols as Reason, Science, Progress. He belonged to that weary, disappointed generation who saw the promises of determinists and scientists unfulfilled, leaving in their train only melancholy, a distaste for life, despair. Joy, he feels, is all the same something different to the sceptical optimism, " the chirping of this library canary called Anatole France."[5] His liberation was slow and difficult, for at first his conversion gave him merely the certitude of the existence of joy but not joy itself. It is this which explains the more feverish, sombre tone of the earliest works which still bear the imprint of disquiet and anguish. Gradually however is revealed the serenity of thought which progresses towards peace. The violence of feelings and passions is attenuated ; the dark atmosphere of bitterness and despair is slowly lightened. Yet there is one striking fact : this progression towards serenity has not diminished the dramatic intensity of conflict. It is merely revealed under a fresh aspect. The struggle now takes place within the heart of man : " Spiritual combat is as brutal as the battle of men."[6] In the midst of his rediscovered peace Claudel was never blind to the tragic and painful aspects of life. He knows that man is ever a wanderer, lost in the

[4] *Ma Conversion. Comment lire Paul Claudel* (Aux Etudiants de France, 1945).
[5] Preface by Claudel to *Anthologie de la Renaissance Catholique*, Vol. I. edited by Louis Chaigne. (" Alsatia," 6th ed.).
[6] Rimbaud. *Oeuvres complètes*, p.201. (Valiquette, Montreal).

heart of a dark forest[7] which encompasses him on all sides and which remains an obstacle between him and the light.

The whole weight of the earth bears down on the characters of the *Tidings* which is the purest, the most serene of Claudel's works. In this mystical drama there is an infinity of human suffering : Pierre is not loved by Violaine ; Mara is not loved by Jacques ; the link between Violaine and Jacques is fragile and shattered by a terrible fate. All remain isolated, even Jacques and Mara, despite their marriage. Earthly desires are frustrated and thwarted.

On the other hand, the world that Claudel paints is a fallen world, marked by original sin. It is clear that Claudel desires, through his plays, to help man, to lead him nearer to God. Yet he does not fall into the error of producing insipid piety, beings where only virtue reigns. If he has created exceptional and pure characters, there is also, as we have seen, a whole procession of those who are guilty of all possible excesses. With an extraordinary strength and a remarkable psychological realism he has depicted the thirst for conquest, the spirit of destruction, selfishness, deceit, the weight of the flesh, pride, hatred and crime. Between these two extremes there is a vast crowd of mediocrities, of " those that are neither hot nor cold ", incapable alike of great sin and of great virtue. Betwixt the heroes and the sinners, " there is the humble pedestrian mass who try in their own way to hold out when they have no means of doing anything else."[8]

[7] This theme of the forest appears very often in Claudel's work. " The forest of trees is that jungle of times, of places, of circumstances, all that natural vegetation which, like Adam, came from ancient paradise, through which the redeeming Will must fray itself a passage, as if with blows of an axe. Each passage thus cut is like a door which opens." *Un Poète regarde la Croix*, p.63. (Gallimard, 24th ed.).

[8] *Ibid*, p.262.

In his own fashion each of Claudel's characters seeks happiness which remains elusive. This is true even of Violaine in the beginning of the *Tidings*. Each being must experience this disappointment in order that he may discover in himself the thirst for something different: " The Claudelian hero, his roots in earth, like a tree, full-blooded, cannot dispense with somebody who is God."[9] In truth, the essence of the Claudelian play is to depict souls, souls which tear themselves away from the passions of the flesh, from the love of conquest or of money. For everything which is limited to earth is threatened by death ; everything which is restricted to the purely human is vanity. Any pursuit of essentially earthly things is doomed to fail :

" And our striving having attained a futile limit
    Undoes itself like a pleat."[10]

Besme[11] repeats ceaselessly: " Nothing is," for despite his power he is solitary and he feels the menace of death. God alone can fill up the abyss which lies before man, thirsty for the infinite. Tête d'Or and later on Rodrigue are obsessed with the futility of conquest ; for Lambert in *La Ville* political ambition becomes empty. Even Cœuvre, the poet, sometimes experiences the limitations of poetry. In *Le Père humilié* Sichel, who had desired so strongly to possess, has with age grown strangely wise. Her only preoccupation is her child, Pensée, whose blindness appears to be the result of a curse on the mother who had wished to deny God and her race. But what the characters must especially realize, in Claudel's plays, is the vanity of earthly love. Because it is

[9] Mauriac, François, 37 (*Revue Intellectuelle*, 1935), p.204. Art. "Quand je dis que j'aime Claudel ".
[10] *Tête d'Or. L'Arbre*, p.164. (Mercure de France, 1901).
[11] *Théâtre*, ii., p.224. (Mercure de France, 1929).

an exclusive, strong, passionate emotion which absorbs all the strength of the individual, there is a danger that it may take the place of the transcendent love which we owe to God. For this reason, in Claudel's plays, that love must be sacrificed, sublimated but not destroyed. Exquisite Dona Musique in the *Satin Slipper* is perhaps the only exception in all Claudel's work. Her tenderness for her husband is so fine and so disinterested, so profoundly spiritual that she experiences even on earth a great and pure happiness.

To relieve the solitude of the majority of his characters, in their inability to discover purely human bliss, Claudel offers them the possibility of an escape towards the supernatural. Man, at once fallen and redeemed, can transcend himself. From the depths of a tragic life he can ascend towards hope. Beside the shadows of sin lies God's grace : a little suffering, the slightest effort towards good, a weakening of pride, can allow it to penetrate : " Christ on the Cross does not cease to toil."[12]

As well as the love of God there is the love of one's fellowmen : the communion of saints. " We are all dying of hunger and thirst. Now in the interior life there are no watertight bulkheads. All hang together. The most mediocre Christian shares the atmosphere breathed by Saint Bernard and Saint John of the Cross."[13] That is why a weak creature can co-operate in the salvation of a fallen tortured world. His sacrifice, his humility, his tears, his prayers can draw towards the light a wretched and suffering humanity, attracted by sin ; can bring back to spiritual realities those

[12] *Un Poète regarde la Croix*, p.243. (Gallimard, 24th ed.).
[13] *Ways and Crossways*, p.242. (Sheed and Ward, 1933).

who have forgotten their soul. Through the action of these chosen beings certain weaknesses will be prevented, certain sins will be confessed and repented of, those who are divided by distrust, jealousy or hatred will know some union in the love of Christ. For these exceptional mortals are of " those who cannot be saved except by saving all that mass which takes its impress in their wake."[14] Their function is to stir souls, to awaken in others the spirit of sacrifice, but not without themselves having borne on their shoulders all the weight of renunciation : " 'Tis you that throw open Paradise to me and you that hinder me from resting there,"[15] moans Rodrigue to Prouhèze who has aroused in him the necessity of, the hunger for a happiness which she forbids. " But soon they perceive that their painful sacrifice . . . has produced inexhaustible consequences."[16] Suffering was essential for the birth of joy.

Claudel's serenity has therefore a distant origin. It does not consist in a selfish isolation or in the self-assuredness of the spiritual *nouveau riche* any more than in false exaltation or naïve illusions. This joy is " the sacrifice of our will."[17] " A Catholic . . . lives in a world of hard realities where he finds himself constrained to make a continual effort."[18] Thus this serenity is a painfully won optimism which must be continually defended, for nothing on this earth can be gained once and for all, eternally. It can issue only from a deeply felt, living faith. It is based on the profound conviction that, despite sin and all the suffering of the earth, God is continually present, watching over all things.

[14] *Satin Slipper*, p.3. (Sheed and Ward, 1931).
[15] *Ibid*, p.132.
[16] P.Claudel, Preface to the stage edition of *Satin Slipper*, p.15. (Gallimard)
[17] *Toi qui es-tu?* p.94. (Gallimard, 3rd ed.).
[18] *Ibid*, p.108.

That is why, all along the rough road, joy remains. It is this unique treasure that the Pope in *Le Père humilié* desired Orian to make known to a tortured world, to these hearts which withdraw and grow hard:

" Make them understand that they have no other duty in the world except joy !

The joy which We know, the joy which We have been charged to give them, make them understand that it is not a vague word, an insipid common-place of the sacristy,

But a horrible, a superb, an absurd, a dazzling, a poignant reality ! and that all the rest is nothing beside it.

Something humble and material and poignant, like the bread which one desires, like the wine which they like so much, like water for lack of which you die if it be not given to you, like fire which burns, like the voice which raises the dead."[19]

[19] *Le Père humilié*, pp.117-8. (Gallimard, 6th ed.).

APPENDIX

i

TETE D'OR

Simon Agnel had left his native country so that he might lead a wandering life in distant lands. With him had gone the girl whom he loved. He returned after many adventures bringing back this dying woman. At the opening of the play he is burying her who had been his companion during his travels. Cébès, a younger man, comes on the scene. He recognizes the woman whom he too had loved ; but he had loved in silence and without hope. The two men, united by this common affection, confide in each other and, because their natures complete each other, they vow friendship. Simon is a leader ; Cébès asks only to be allowed to give. Simon, the strong man, feels his powerlessness and weakness when faced by death but, since his soul is " impatient and wild ", he is determined to try whether he can conquer the world.

In the second part of the play we are in a palace. Disorder is everywhere, for Barbarians are attacking the kingdom and the only hope of the king and of the state lies in an adventurer whose shining hair has won for him the name of " Tête d'Or "—Simon. From a crowd of frightened beings Tête d'Or has made an army and the decisive battle is being waged. In the palace Cébès, dying, has been left in the charge of the king by Simon. That night, a few men await the issue of the combat which they believe to be already lost. The Princess, symbol of beauty and joy, appears for a moment in this scene of despair. She measures the defeatism of these men and, having tried in vain to console Cébès, she too feels the common fear : she is a poor, powerless woman.

At dawn comes the news : Tête d'Or has been victorious. He returns but his achievement arouses in him no joy ;

his only thought is of Cébès who dies, thus giving to Simon a foretaste of man's fundamental vulnerability.

After Cébès' death, Tête d'Or, although he feels the vanity of the desire for possessions, cannot prevent himself from aspiring to supreme power. By virtue of his strength alone he claims the right to rule, offering to his fellows not peace and plenty, but war and conquest with him as their leader. The old king is killed, the Princess is driven away and Tete d'Or's reign begins.

In the third part of the play the scene is laid at the utmost limits of Europe, in the Caucasus where Tête d'Or has led his army. At the moment when he is about to begin his last battle which will make him master of the entire continent, he gives a crust which he had kept for this day to a wretched beggar woman . . . A deserter takes the bread from her and recognizes her as the Princess. Hating, with the hatred of petty envy, the joy and loveliness which she represents, he insults her and nails her by her hands to a tree.

Meanwhile the army had been put to flight. Tête d'Or, however, had continued to fight alone. Mortally wounded he fell but his cry rallied the fleeing soldiers. The leader himself is borne unconscious up the mountain but victory is won.

Recovering consciousness, Simon realizes the emptiness of all that for which he strove. He had wished to possess the earth but he now realizes the powerlessness of man when he desires to substitute himself for God.

Having been left alone to die at his own wish, he hears a cry and sees the Princess, crucified. By a great effort he frees her. Instead of hating this man who had killed her father and driven her from the throne she pardons him and reveals her love for him. Before dying he proclaims her queen. But she too dies. The now leaderless soldiers retreat towards their native land bearing with them only the dead body of their queen.

ii

LA VILLE

The play opens in the gardens of Isidore de Besme, the master of the Town. On him, the engineer, depends its whole life which has been reduced to a purely material level. Lambert, his weaker brother, directs the politics of the Town for, since all revealed religion is long since dead, man requires a plaything which may serve as a substitute. Avare, like Tête d'Or, a man of mysterious origin, represents the spirit of destruction. He is a man of violence, capable of organizing revolt and of casting down the entire social order. To him Lambert confides that he hopes soon to marry his ward, Lâla.

Meanwhile a revolt is beginning in the Town and Avare, full of joy, does all in his power to make men more conscious of the slavery in which they exist. Lâla agrees to marry the old man, Lambert, for she as yet knows nothing of love. A dialogue between Besme and Coeuvre compares the art of the engineer to that of the poet. While Coeuvre feels the wonder of nature, Besme is overwhelmed by the thought of the futility of all things. Like Tête d'Or, who had learned the vanity of conquest, Besme learns the emptiness of science.

Lâla announces to them her forthcoming marriage but she feels herself suddenly attracted by Coeuvre's youth. Lambert, whose love has made him leave aside politics, agrees to resume his task of governing only if Lâla renews her promise. But she has turned towards the poet, who, until then, had desired only solitude and his art. In face of Lambert's persistency, Lâla, despite her promise, casts herself at Coeuvre's feet. The poet yields and leads away Lâla whom he will marry.

In the second Act the characters have gathered together in a cemetery. Lambert, rejected by life, has consecrated himself to the dead and has become a grave-digger. Avare's task has been accomplished : all work has ceased in the Town and man has risen from his slavery. Lâla, having left Coeuvre to whom she has given a son, now lives with Avare.

She tries in vain to rekindle in Lambert the desire to live, for her rôle as a woman is to create, not to destroy. For this reason she understands better than Avare the needs of these men in revolt who have abandoned their work.

Besme is in despair because men no longer accomplish their daily task and nevertheless he remains convinced of the nothingness of all things. Lambert, who has listened to his brother's tragic words, looks for the last time on the beauty and the youth of Lâla, and goes away to die.

Lâla then explains to Besme, although without convincing him, that man, however abject and wretched he may be, can unite with his fellows to form a harmonious whole. Coeuvre whose aid she asks for the construction of the new Town, refuses " to handle men's souls as if they were bricks." Then Lâla, changing her attitude, begs Avare to spare the old Town and to respect the work of the past ; that violent man remains however subject to the impulse of the moment.

In the distance, the Town is given over to the flames and its destruction is accomplished. " All is finished," says Avare. He goes out, followed by Lâla. Besme and Coeuvre remain alone in the cemetery. Besme knows that he is about to die ; he realizes that his life has been a failure and, once again, he measures the powerlessness of science. He goes out to die at the hands of the rebels.

The third Act takes place years later. Avare has achieved supreme power, but he is a man of destruction ; he is incapable of rebuilding the shattered Town. Having no further function to perform, he goes away, no one knows whither, leaving Ivors, the son of Coeuvre and Lâla, to take his place. This Prince is anxious to serve the interests of the Town, to help his people, but he feels that man aspires to something higher than earthly prosperity. It is at this moment that Coeuvre returns. He has become a Bishop and is followed by his priests. The poet, whom nothing had ever completely satisfied, has at last found God. Ivors, who at first resists this " old superstition ", yields at last, won over by his father's conversion and by the beauty of the message which he brings. In his own name and in that of his people the Prince accepts the *Credo*. Lâla appears, now an old, grey-haired woman. Ivors wishes to reject her, for she bears a share of responsibility for this Town in ruins. But she, who feels that death is near, reminds him of the rôle of woman and of her place amongst men. It is she who awakens in man a desire for that which surpasses him, for that which surpasses all earthly things. She goes away and Ivors prepares to face the reconstruction of the new Town.

iii

L'ECHANGE

A young American, Louis Laine, who has Indian blood in his veins, has married a Frenchwoman, Marthe, and has taken her across the ocean. Absolute freedom, freedom as an end not as a means, is his only desire and, at the beginning of the play, he has no longer any use for this woman whom he has married. Marthe, on the other hand, is his antithesis ; she is the quiet woman of duty, reliable and loving. She is not made for the wandering life which alone seems possible to Louis ; her heart aches in exile. She is made to serve and now she feels that Louis has no longer any need of her. She has become a barrier betwixt the world and him ; he dreams only of escape. Even when he assures Marthe that he loves no other woman, her disquiet is not relieved.

The house in which the couple dwell belongs to a rich merchant, Thomas Pollock, and it is close to the property of this man of business. He has somewhere, he does not quite know where, a wife and daughter, but he is living with an actress, Léchy Elbernon. One morning they both come to visit Louis Laine's house and Thomas Pollock, for a moment alone with Marthe, suggests to her that she leave her husband. When the other two return a conversation between the two women reveals the fundamental contrast between their characters. Marthe represents truth and fidelity ; Léchy, error and all those traits which separate human beings one from the other.

When they go off together Thomas Pollock offers Louis a handful of dollars for Marthe. To him, a merchant, obsessed by commerce, seeing all things in the light of their monetary value, such an "exchange" appears quite permissible. Is not Marthe the property of her husband? After a slight hesitation Louis who needs money and who desires his liberty, accepts the bargain. The situation existing amidst these four people is now ready to allow the climax.

In Act II Louis, because the bargain must be fulfilled, attempts to pick a quarrel with Marthe. It would simplify his problem a lot if she would leave him of her own free will. He overwhelms her with reproaches, and shows her that she was wrong to marry a foreigner such as himself, good for nothing, incapable of providing for a wife ; on the other hand, Thomas Pollock could make her very happy. Marthe, discovering his aim, cries out in horror. She feels that not she alone but all her race is thus outraged. For the last time she strives to make him see the beauty and the wonder of marriage, but in vain. Léchy then comes to aid him and reveals to Marthe that Louis is already her lover. Louis admits his weakness ; he knows that what he does is evil but he loves Léchy. The actress presents to him two pictures : the freedom which she symbolizes and duty which is personified by Marthe. Louis chooses ; speaking of Léchy, he says to Marthe : " It is she whom I love." Marthe then bids a solemn good-bye to her husband. In the concluding scene of this act Léchy and Louis are alone. The actress, who genuinely loves him, is suddenly afraid that he will abandon her too. Louis, however, in casting aside Marthe, has also cast aside life ; for the first time he feels that death is close.

In Act III we find Marthe alone at night, near the sea. In her sorrow she calls on the Universe and on God for justice. She weeps at the thought of her exile ; she sees in her mind the well-loved, familiar scenes of her native land and she cries out in her solitude. Léchy, who is drunk, comes at this moment when Marthe has lost all and brings her the temptation of despair. She suggests to her three methods of escape : to kill herself ; to kill Louis or to be killed by Léchy. But Marthe is a force of life, not of destruction. Léchy then shows how she will kill Louis should he attempt to leave her ; for she knows how slight is her hold on him. She will be able too to ruin Thomas Pollock by burning the house which contains his whole fortune. Marthe is in no way troubled by these threats ; it is the actress who weakens and who begs her to persuade Louis to remain.

Louis, obscurely drawn, comes to Marthe. She can no longer save him ; he had desired solitude and his salvation must come from himself. Only if he agreed to give back the money of the " exchange " to Thomas Pollock could her help be of any avail to him now ; this he refuses to do. After his departure, Thomas Pollock comes; his attitude has changed ; he now wishes merely to apologize and to talk to her for a few moments. Face to face with this upright honest woman, the hard merchant studies himself and relives his past : Marthe has made him understand that he too possesses a soul. His house blazes ; he is ruined. The thought hardly worries him, he sees life in a new perspective. A shot is then heard. Léchy, drunk, appears. Having shot Louis, she sings and dances on the stage.

Marthe explains to Thomas Pollock that his duty is now to look after Léchy. She herself has no movement of revolt. She accepts her solitude and Louis' death, since that is God's will.

iv

PARTAGE DE MIDI

On a vessel bound for China, Ysé, estranged from her husband, the weak de Ciz, meets Mesa. This profoundly sad man, while he was in Europe, had sought, as he believed in vain, a call from God. Ysé is a passionate woman, whose nature is potentially very rich, but the wandering life which she has led with her selfish husband has made her willing to accept any risk, any change. On board there is also a very resolute but somewhat brutal man, Almaric, an adventurer. Before her marriage he had known Ysé, and now he tries in vain to awaken her interest in him anew. Ysé is attracted by Mesa. The solitude of that silent man, the midday hour, " midday in the heavens, midday in our lives ", as he says, this woman who is ready to give up everything for him—all this exposes him to temptation. Ysé, who obscurely senses his nobility and the presence in him of something intensely spiritual, is suddenly moved by fear for she feels that the idea of becoming his mistress is almost sacriligious.

The second Act is unfolded in the European cemetery of Hong-Kong. Ysé is going to meet Mesa again. While he awaits her arrival he knows, with a terrible lucidity, that he has already sinned in his heart. He moves aside and Ysé arrives with Ciz. This adventurer is about to depart on a journey which will, he hopes, enrich him ; he will be absent for about a month. Ysé asks him not to go ; although he realizes the danger to which she is exposed, he persists in his intention. Thus, Ysé, whose soul has for years been closed to Grace, sees herself deprived of her last support.

When Ysé and Mesa find themselves alone together their fall is inevitable. He, because he is unable to interpret God's call, feels himself abandoned ; she has just been deserted by the man whose duty it was to protect her. They fall into each other's arms. Mesa chooses Ysé instead of God. But their passion is joyless ; they each experience a sense of solitude. They feel, especially Mesa, that true union between souls is impossible in guilty love.

In the last scene of Act II Ciz asks for Mesa's advice about his journey ; the latter, while in fact doing all he can to encourage Ciz to depart, hypocritically pretends that he wishes him to remain.

Just as Mesa could not give himself entirely to God, so a part of him escapes Ysé. Nevertheless this tragic love lasts for a year ; then Ysé, who has an intense capacity for life, turns her back on this passion which resembles death. She goes to Almaric, the man who, humanly speaking she should have married, for they were made for each other. Bearing Mesa's child she becomes Almaric's mistress. She has abandoned her children and lives with him on his prosperous plantation.

A rising takes place and the Chinese massacre the Europeans. Almaric, to ensure that they will not be taken alive, has laid an explosive which will set fire to the house during the night. Ysé has no fear of death. She thinks now of Ciz whom she has deceived, of her children whom she has abandoned, of Mesa whom she has betrayed. Since she met Mesa she has known that there is something else as well as carnal love ; her conscience has been awakened ; she feels ashamed. While she is alone preparing herself for death, Mesa comes and offers her life : he has a pass, Ciz is dead and they can marry. Ysé does not answer, it is too late and she is vowed to death. Mesa, exasperated by her silence, is even tempted to kill her but he then understands that she has been unable to pardon him for one thing : his inability to give his soul unreservedly to her while they were together. He wishes to save their child at least, but Ysé remains obstinately silent. Almaric returns and asks Ysé to make a sign if she wishes to escape ; she remains motionless. Mesa makes a threatening gesture and Almaric disarms him and strikes him so that he lies unconscious on the ground. Ysé tells Almaric to take the pass from Mesa ; she goes in to look at the child, and returns to say that he is dead : she has strangled him. She has, she thinks, made her choice : life with Almaric instead of death with Mesa.

Mesa, abandoned, regains consciousness. He repents, for he knows that he had been destined to save Ysé whereas he had led her into sin. He at last sees God's designs ; he accepts death and relies on God's love to save him.

At the moment of going on board ship, Ysé had turned back, and she returns to this house which is doomed to destruction. Her final choice is made. Her only duty now is to be at the side of this man who has lost all and who awaits certain death. The union of midnight has replaced the union of midday and, she says to Mesa, " Here I am, ready to be freed."

L'OTAGE (¹)

This play has its setting in the years 1812-1814. Georges de Coûfontaine is an *émigré* who, in order to serve his king, has been absent from his country for twenty years. His wife, who had been unfaithful to him with the Dauphin, and his two children have all three died of fever. Despite all, Georges continues to serve, even though he knows that his efforts will be vain, for times have changed. He and his cousin, Sygne, are the last of his family. Sygne, who had remained in France, had in spite of great difficulties, restored the family property.

Attracted to each other by their common misfortune and by their pride in their race, the two cousins take a solemn oath proclaiming their engagement. Despite their profound union, their attitude towards religion is very different. Georges no longer believes, whereas Sygne has a fervent faith. Their marriage, which both so eagerly desired, might have restored their family. But, while Napoleon is at Moscow, Georges has helped Pope Pius VII to escape from his prison and brings him to Coûfontaine.

Toussaint Turelure, Prefect, Baron of the Empire, represents the new age. His father had been a sorcerer; his mother, an excellent, pious woman, had seconded Sygne's efforts to restore the fortunes of the family. He it was who delivered up to the executioner the parents of Georges and those of Sygne. His dream now is to possess Coûfontaine and to marry this young girl who represents for him that which is most desirable and most difficult to conquer. He knows that the Pope is a guest at Coûfontaine, and he presents to Sygne a terrible choice : either she must marry Turelure, or else the Pope will be sent back to captivity.

Sygne at first indignantly rejects the proposal of this man who is responsible for the death of her parents. The priest,

(¹) *L'Otage*, *Le Pain dur* and *Le Père humilié* form a trilogy which deals with the period between 1812 and 1871.

Badilon, however, gradually convinces her that she must sacrifice herself. He in no way forces her decision : God does not ask, in justice, that she deliver herself up as a hostage to save the Pope. He reminds her, however, of all that Christ suffered. Sygne, heart-broken, ends her engagement to Georges and agrees to marry Turelure.

Two years later Sygne has a son and Turelure has been made Prefect of Seine. Now that Napoleon's fall is imminent, this opportunist is ready to hand over Paris to Louis XVIII. He lays down only two conditions : Georges de Coûfontaine must make over his property to Turelure's son and the King must accept the *Charte* and reign as a constitutional monarch.

Georges accepts and he is sent by the King to negotiate. He attempts however to avenge himself on Turelure. He shoots ; but Toussaint was on the watch and fires at the same moment, killing Georges ; the bullet, aimed at him, strikes Sygne who had thrown herself in front of her husband. The young woman, dying, does not yet seem ready to pardon him and it is he, the cruel cynical man, who in vain implores her forgiveness. Even his appeal to her religion has no effect. He then calls on her in the name of the motto of her family *Coûfontaine adsum*. This affects her ; Sygne makes a last gesture which can be interpreted as one of pardon.

vi

LE PAIN DUR

The play opens in the one-time library of Coûfontaine. The great bronze crucifix which Sygne had saved has been taken down and in its place there is a portrait of Louis-Philippe. Turelure has remained avid both of money and of love. Lumîr, a Polish Countess, and Sichel, a Jewess and Turelure's mistress, discuss the possibility of obtaining a sum of money from the old man. Lumîr wishes him to give her ten thousand francs, which she had lent to Louis, the son of Sygne and Turelure ; she also desires a further ten thousand as this will enable Louis to work the land in Africa which he loves so much and which by his unremitting toil he has at last made productive. But Toussaint hates this son who reminds him of Sygne and who, moreover, by his avidity for possessions, is rather too much his own portrait. Acting through Sichel's father, a usurer, he has ruined his son who had been forced to borrow money at a high rate of interest. He knows that Louis, overburdened with debt, will be forced to yield the land to him, and that he himself will thus obtain a good bargain.

Sichel, who is bitter with the bitterness of a despised race, wishes to marry a Christian. She has chosen Louis with whom she has been in correspondence about his business transactions. She therefore fears Lumîr who is engaged to Louis. She soon discovers however that only one thing is of any real importance to the little Countess : Poland and the money which she had lent to Louis, since that money came from a fund which had been destined to aid her country. Sichel incites Lumîr to murder Toussaint. Lumîr, in return for Sichel's help, offers to return to Poland and so to leave the way free, after the old man's death, for a marriage between the Jewess and Louis.

Turelure agrees to give Lumîr the money on condition that she marry him. Meanwhile Louis has been warned by Sichel and his arrival is imminent. The Jewess, playing on Toussaint's fear of being murdered either for his money or because he has attempted to steal his son's fiancée, induces him to draw up documents which make it appear that all his property belongs to her and her father. His hatred of his son, his desire to obtain Lumîr, cause him thus to deliver himself into the hands of his most dangerous enemy.

After Louis' return, Lumîr with infinite skill conveys to him the impression that, from necessity, she will marry his father in order to obtain her money. She proves to him too that he will not be able to pay interest which will shortly fall due, and that his only means of escape is to threaten his father and, if that fails, to get rid of the old man. After some hesitation Louis accepts. She gives him two pistols, telling him that, while one is loaded, the other is not. Fear alone, she says, having taken the hint from Sichel, will suffice to kill Toussaint.

The interview between the father and son throws a tragic light on these two men who, fundamentally, are very much alike. Louis begs Toussaint to allow him at least to work the soil which now, after all his toil, is ready and which he loves. He meets with a refusal. He offers to accept merely the money which he owes to Lumîr. Again his father refuses : if Lumîr had the money he would have no further hold over her. Louis, driven to despair, shoots with both pistols. Lumîr had lied when she said that one pistol was not loaded. Nevertheless, both shots miss. The old man, however, dies of shock.

Turelure leaves apparently very little money but Lumîr obtains what was owed to her. She will not marry Louis. She does not love him enough to accompany him to Africa and he, on his side, lets her set out alone for Poland, that "fatherland of sorrow". She is going towards her own countrymen who have lost all and to whom she will bring the love which Louis did not want.

Sichel destroys the paper which made over all Turelure's property to her and to her father. Louis who, despite everything, is of Coûfontaine blood, cannot accept this generosity without giving to the Jewess in return that which she desires : he therefore asks her to marry him. Then, having given up to his future father-in-law the ancient domain of Coûfontaine, he sells to him for four francs the kilogramme the old bronze figure of Christ which years before his mother had saved, when she walked bare-footed the whole night, carrying it in her arms and praying.

vii

LE PERE HUMILIE

The play opens during a masked party held at the Villa Wronski in Rome, in May, 1869.

Louis Turelure, an opportunist like his father, is the Ambassador of Napoleon III at the Vatican. Sichel has aged and she has known sorrow. Her only daughter, Pensée, has been blind from birth ; it seems as if she were paying for the sin of her parents. Her infirmity is all the more pitiful because she is beautiful, sensitive and greatly gifted. In these gardens full of the scent of Spring she wears the costume of Autumn. Her sense of hearing is so highly developed that she enjoys the loveliness around her as keenly as if she could see. In fact, she finds her way so well that nobody guesses she is blind. She loves Orian de Homodarmes, whose voice she recognizes among all others, but she loves him without much hope for her infirmity makes it unlikely that she will be sought in marriage. As well, her mother is a Jewess and her father, from a political and religious point of view, represents everything which Orian and his brother Orso most detest. Pensée herself is Christian in name only ; the two brothers are nephews of the Pope and Orian is his god-son. Orso however is in love with her and he has asked his brother— who is also secretly in love—to speak to her for him. This Orian has agreed to do in the hope that thus he will raise an impassible barrier between himself and her.

When Orian and Pensée are alone together, however, they know before a word is spoken that they love each other. They are made for each other ; they complete each other. In her, even spiritually, all is shadows and she awaits a light which Orian alone can bring her. How could he resist the call of this soul which cries to him for support? To him she reveals her blindness, for there must be no secret between them.

When Orso discovers their mutual love he refuses to profit by his brother's generosity. Finally they agree to accept the decision of their uncle whose heart is torn by the attacks on the Papacy.

In the second Act, the Pope, " Le Père humilié," confides in a humble friar ; he tells of his sorrow at the sight of waning faith, of the blasphemy and despair of men without

God. It is at this hour of depression that the two brothers come to ask him to decide their difficult case. For each other's sake, they both wish to renounce this girl whom they both love. Orso, the soldier, wishes Orian to marry Pensée because she loves him. Orian, who knows that he has had a call from God, realizes that he cannot give to her that which is most genuine in him : " She does not ask for my light, she would like to share her night with me." Moreover, there is the Pope whom all abandon, and who speaks to him of the other blind people in the world who await the light, of all the unhappy beings who must be taught that faith in and love of God mean Joy.

Orian leaves. He goes on a voyage and spends a year along the African coast. Orso at last becomes officially engaged to Pensée for he is convinced that with time he will be able to win her love.

Act III takes place in September, 1870, just after the revolution. Orian returns from the wanderings by which he has tried in vain to rid himself of the memory of Pensée. Both young men are going to fight for France in the Franco-Prussian War. Orso arranges a meeting between his brother and his fiancée. Orian no longer strives to hide his love : she must be his, not Orso's. Pensée, in virtue of the sacrifice which Sygne made years before for the Pope, claims her rights over Orian. Since he is about to leave, since she is so beautiful and so frail, since she mentions the old debt, Orian yields completely to his love. In his weakness, he is even ready to remain with her, to neglect his duty ; it is Pensée who bids him go. We learn later that they saw each other once more before Orian's departure : " a wordless, tragic meeting, like people who have reached the limit of endurance and who no longer know what they are doing."

The last Act is in January, 1871. Pensée is going to have a child. No letter has been received from Orian. Orso arrives bearing the news of his death ; he died, begging his brother to ask Pensée's forgiveness for him. She had foreseen this death and she knows that now Orian has rediscovered the liberty and the light towards which his whole being tended. She will marry Orso, such was Orian's wish: Orian's child must not be deprived of his birthright.

viii

THE SATIN SLIPPER

(This play, almost certainly Claudel's greatest work, is, because of its ampleness, extremely difficult to synopsize. Instead of being divided into Acts it is laid in four " Days " of uncertain length. To use Claudel's own words : " The Scene of this play is the world, and more especially Spain at the close of the Sixteenth, unless it be the opening of the Seventeenth, Century." It is a period full of life : the time of the great discoveries, of the wonders of Michael Angelo, of the gallant courage of Don John of Austria. And against this back-cloth move the two chief characters of the play : Don Rodrigue and Dona Prouhèze).

In the opening scene a Jesuit, dying alone, in mid-ocean, prays God to save his brother, Rodrigue de Manacor, who, like Tête d'Or, is full of ambition. He begs God to bring his brother back to Him by inspiring in Rodrigue a love which in this life will know no satisfaction.

Prouhèze, who appears in the next scene, had previously met Rodrigue. She tells Don Balthazar, asked by her husband to escort her on a long journey, that she loves this man whom she had only seen for a short time. Her husband, a grave austere judge, is much older than she and he inspires her with the mingled emotions of fear and respect. She knows that her love for Rodrigue can have no issue, for she is not free, and that, moreover, her becoming his mistress could not satisfy their hearts. She realizes, however, the weakness of human nature so, at the moment of leaving her husband's house, she turns to the statue of the Virgin who guards its threshold and lays in those outstretched hands one of her satin slippers ; and she prays that thus, should she take the road towards evil, her walk may be halting and lame.

Rodrigue, on his side, has conceived for Prouhèze a love which nothing can extinguish. He suffers during his absence from her and longs to rejoin her. Yet, passionate though this love is, it is far from being purely carnal. He explains to his Chinese servant : " What I love in her is not at all what can be dissolved and escape me and be far away, and some time cease to love me."

The Virgin heard Prouhèze's prayer. Rodrigue, preparing in answer to a letter from her to join her, is seriously wounded. Prouhèze escapes to meet him but when she reaches the castle where Rodrigue's mother is nursing her son, she does not even see him ; her husband, Don Pélage, arrives. He understands the suffering of his wife ; but no understanding can alter the one unchangeable fact : their marriage is an indissoluble link. He finds a remedy, " instead of a temptation, a greater temptation." Prouhèze accepts the difficult task which Pélage suggests : she will assume command of the fort at Mogador in Morocco with, as lieutenant, Don Camille, who loves her passionately and who had previously declared this love to her. She agrees because she is ardent and proud, and because she loves Africa and the dangerous difficult life which she will lead.

Rodrigue, meantime, has been chosen by the King of Spain to be Viceroy of the Americas. He accepts, but only on condition that Prouhèze be not left at Mogador. The King orders him to go himself and to tell her that she is free to return to Spain should she so desire. Prouhèze refuses to see him, merely sending a message that she intends to remain. She thus chooses to stay on with Don Camille whom she does not love, while sending away the man whom she adores. By chance that evening the two meet. In complete silence they stand and, beneath the rays of the moon, their two shadows for an instant are merged into one on the white wall, but quickly they part. Prouhèze understands that, through his great and unsatisfied love for her, this man will be led towards God.

Years pass, during which Rodrigue accomplishes his marvellous task in Spanish America, yet without having been able to forget for an instant the woman whom he loves. Meanwhile Don Pélage has died. Prouhèze sends out a call to Rodrigue, for Don Camille is urging her to marry him. The letter, which seems to bring ill-fortune to all those to whom it is entrusted, takes ten years to reach him. Immediately on receiving it, Rodrigue leaves for Mogador, but he arrives too late. Prouhèze, in order to preserve the territory for Spain, has had to marry Don Camille who is a renegade. God has demanded that her sacrifice be complete. If the love of Prouhèze and of Rodrigue had been, from the earthly view-point, happy, it would have failed in its object. As it is, Prouhèze's sacrifice may save not only herself and the man who loves her but also, perhaps, Don Camille. This she explains to Rodrigue during their last meeting which takes place on his ship. She refuses to leave with him, but has decided to return as she had promised to Don Camille and, as she knows, to death. That night, to forestall a last attack by the Moors the citadel will be blown up and there will perish Prouhèze, Camille and the garrison. This scene is the most poignant of the whole play. Rodrigue does not yet understand the full meaning of the words by which Prouhèze explains to him that she will disappear from this world, but will remain the " eternal star " for which he will thirst. At the end, Rodrigue weeps but he lets her go. To him however she entrusts her and Camille's daughter.

The scene of the " Fourth Day " is laid at sea. We learn that, after the death of Prouhèze, Rodrigue had set out for Japan ; he had been shipwrecked, lost a leg in battle and spent several years in a Japanese prison. He then returned to Spain, where he found himself out of favour at the Court. When we see him he is dressed in rags, but he remains proud and mocking. He earns his living by painting holy pictures which he sells to the fisher folk. One single being remains dear to him, Dona Sept Epées, Prouhèze's child and his adopted daughter. This man in his poverty and suffering is still very close to Prouhèze. The memory of his love tortures him : " My soul is empty ", he tells Dona Sept Epées, "because of her who is not here." Dona Sept Epées is an intrepid being who goes by the most direct path to that which she deems best. Although she has not mentioned it to Rodrigue, she is in love with Don John of Austria. This episode takes us back to the beginning of the play, for Don John is the son of Dona Musica, an exquisite being, who was at the inn when Prouhèze learnt of Rodrigue's injury. Dona Musica had fled from home to avoid a loveless marriage, for she knew, with absolute certainty, that she would one day wed the King of Naples whom she had never even met. After many adventures, she landed in Sicily, and, as in a fairy story, met him, married him and gave him a son. Sept Epées curiously enough resembles her : she has the same calm certitude before love and life, but she has also something of the passionate nature of her mother. She wishes to follow Don John in his Crusade against Islam and tries to induce Rodrigue to accompany her. He however has other plans. Incorrect news has been received in Spain that the Armada has been victorious and the King wishes him to govern England. He had refused once. Then an actress, by the King's orders, pretends to be Mary Stuart ; she comes to Rodrigue, throws herself at his feet and implores him to assist her. Together they work out a plan of government. When he arrives at the Court he is alone in not knowing that the Armada has been defeated. He states his acceptance of the King's offer, but he lays down certain conditions which consider Spanish interests less than those of international politics : England must be given free access to the riches of Spanish America.

Mocked by the Court and declared a traitor, Rodrigue is sold as a slave. In chains on the boat he has to submit to the insults, the jeers, the brutality of the two soldiers who lead him away. Now for the first time, when all is lost, even liberty, does he feel himself really free. At last the plans of Providence are clear to him. Sept Epées has left with Don John for the Crusades ; he has no ties on earth. He is handed scornfully over to the Carmelites of Saint Teresa ; he will live the remainder of his life as a porter in one of their convents.

The play finishes with words which evoke not only the victory of Lepanto but also Rodrigue's new-found peace : " Deliverance to souls in prison."